Heaven
On Earth
FAMILY STYLE

Abundant Living Ministries
Lititz, PA

ISBN-13: 978-0-9759019-1-5
ISBN-10: 0-9759019-1-5

Abundant Living Ministries
541 W 28th Division Hwy
Lititz, PA 17543
AbundantLivingMinistries.org
email: info@AbundantLivingMinistries.org

Printed in the United States of America
Library of Congress Catalog Card Number: 80-84230
International Standard Book Number: 0-914903-97-7
Abundant Living Ministries, Lititz, PA

Contents

Dedication

To my dear wife, Betty, who has been a true helpmate, encouraging me to become what I am today.

Also to my children and grandchildren, for all their loving cooperation, understanding and encouragement.

Special thanks to our daughter-in-law, Sharon, who worked so diligently and sweetly to help us share our story.

Foreword

When Betty and I read the final draft of this story, we were deeply moved. As we reflected on all God had done for us, our hearts overflowed with gratitude. We couldn't wait to share all the wonderful things that had happened to us. We wanted to relate the many answers to prayer we had witnessed. Then someone asked us, "Are all your prayers answered?" Of course not! But when we don't see the answer, we still keep on thanking and loving Jesus.

Our oldest son Jim, asked his mother if she could stay with their two older children while his wife Charlotte, would be in the hospital with the new baby, due in a couple of months. Yes! This would indeed be a privilege, so we began making plans. However, Betty discovered that the only week she was totally free was the week of May 24, and that was ten days before the due date. Betty asked, "Charlotte, do you believe it would be all right to pray that your baby will be born on May 24?"

Charlotte thought about it a few moments and said, "Yes, I believe we could do that."

We joined hands, and I simply asked the Lord to please bring the baby on May 24. Betty said, "Now, Charlotte, we need to act like we believe it." Well, she went further than we really expected! As her doctor was finishing her monthly checkup the following week, she announced, "The baby is going to be born on May 24."

He asked, "Why do you say that? That would be ten days early."

She replied, "That's the only week it suits my mother-in-law to stay with our children, and we prayed about it and we are believing God." She stuck her neck out, didn't she?

The night before this was to happen, Betty called her, "How are you, Charlotte? Do you have any symptoms?" "No I don't," she replied. "But I'll go tomorrow."

Early the next morning, the telephone rang. It was Jim. "Dad," he began, "tell Mother to come down. I'm taking Charlotte to the hospital." That day a beautiful baby boy, Matthew, was born to happy parents.

You may ask, "What would you have done if that had not happened?" Do you know what we do at a time like that? We thank and love the Lord anyway. We do not love and serve Him only for what He does for us, but for who He is.

This same Lord loves you! He cares about you! He knows you by your first name; He even knows how many hairs you have on your head. In other words, He has a personal interest in you! You are special to Him!

Several months before this book was published, some of our prayer partners began praying for a special blessing on everyone who will read this story. We are believing together that something good is going to happen to you!

J. Norman Charles

July 1980

Preface

When I first began interviewing Dad and Mom for this book, Mom commented, "Sharon, you're either going to like us more after this ordeal, or wish you'd never met us!" I laughed then and I'm still laughing.

Norman and Betty Charles are the kind of people who win your respect the first time you meet them and never lose it.

When I began dating their son John, I remember vividly our first long walk together. We arrived at the bank of a meandering stream and plunked down on the grass to chat. I knew absolutely nothing of John's background and was eager to learn all I could.

As he shared some of the fond memories and incredible events of his childhood, my curiosity was aroused. This Charles family had to be one-of-a-kind! I hoped in my heart that God would give me the opportunity to meet his parents someday.

Little did I realize that eventually God would unite me with John and plunge us into daily contact with his folks!

They are delightful people! They devote themselves tirelessly to helping others. Their sparkling humor, endless energy and enthusiasm, and sincere compassion for others, make them a joy to be with and a challenging example to follow! Norm and Betty would be the first to admit they weren't always this way! The more I discovered about the painful first thirteen years of their marriage, the more wonder I felt about the transforming power of God's Holy Spirit! That He could take them from what they were, to what they became, is a soul-stirring miracle!

But you can discover that for yourself! It's their story— a story which has served only to make me love them more!

Sharon Charles

1

Milking Stool Memories

"No! I will not! Norm, I just can't get out of bed today! I feel terrible! Go away and leave me alone!" Betty turned over in bed, yanked angrily at the sheets and disappeared under the bed covers.

I turned away with a sigh and headed out to the barn. It was the summer of 1957 and I had a lot of work to do on our 120-acre Lancaster County farm. No use to stand around and argue. I knew from experience that when my wife got into one of these moods, nothing I could do or say would coax her into action.

Trouble was, these moods were getting more and more frequent. She seemed so depressed, refusing to move from her bed for days at a time. For me, this meant calling in one of her sisters or a local Mennonite girl to take care of our five young children plus the household chores. It meant no help with the garden, or gathering eggs, or bringing in the milk. It meant getting into bed at night, dead-tired, only to hear Betty's complaining and criticizing for another hour or so. I know it irritated her that I refused to respond—I seldom even got angry with her. At least outwardly I didn't. The fact was, I felt extremely upset with her, but I was just too tired to retaliate. Plus my strict upbringing had molded me into a timid, reserved man who rarely expressed his real feelings on anything.

As I entered the big white barn that morning my thoughts were troubling me. I loved Betty, but I was at my wit's end. I just didn't know what to do with her anymore. We'd tried going to all sorts of doctors and I knew that apart from a few headaches and minor pains, she was okay. But the words of the last doctor kept haunting me.

"It's no use, Mr. Charles," he had said kindly, "your wife would be better off in an institution." I knew what kind of institution he was talking about, and to me the word conjured up terrifying thoughts of screaming people, padded walls and isolation.

"She's too stubborn to agree to that!" I argued. "There must be some other way to help her."

"We've all done our best to help your wife. I don't think you have much choice. Just tell her you're taking her for a ride some Sunday afternoon, and then drop her off at the hospital." I guess he read the sadness in my heart at that moment, for he added gently as I turned to go, "I'm sorry, Norm. I really am."

I sat down wearily on the milking stool and rested my head on my hands. "Milking can wait a little longer today. I just have to get my thoughts sorted out first. I have to make a decision.

"How could I put Betty away in some mental hospital? I love her so much! True, she hasn't been much of a wife lately, but we have been through so much together. It would tear me up to be separated from the only girl I have ever loved."

It made me smile a bit to think back to when we first met...

We had both grown up in Lancaster County Mennonite families and had attended church most of our lives. In the spring this always meant we would attend area revival meetings every night for a week or so. When Spring Revival of 1941 rolled around, my buddies and I held a little conference before the first service.

"What do you say if we all have ourselves dates by the end of revival?" I suggested hesitantly, trying to hide my own uncertainty. I was very shy and I wasn't sure I'd have the courage to ask any girl to go out with me. But I was also too embarrassed to admit my fears. I wanted to impress my friends, I guess.

My pal, Harry, was quick to reply, "Suits me fine! It's about time you started thinking about girls, Norm! I was beginning to wonder if you'd ever start dating. After all, your folks made you promise not to date till you were eighteen, but you're eighteen and a half now and you still haven't had one date! What's been keeping you? You scared or something?"

Well, he was sure right there, but I couldn't let on that he had guessed my problem, so I made up my mind fast. "Of course I'm not scared—I just haven't seen any girl that interests me yet."

3

"Well, look them over tonight during the meeting. There are a lot of nice-looking girls here this year. I've already got mine picked out, so whatever you do, don't choose her!"

"I won't," I promised. I knew I'd have to have a date chosen by the end of the week, or I'd be teased unmercifully. After all, it had been my suggestion. What a dumb idea!

When we filed into church that evening my mind was certainly not on the sermon. I could hardly tell you a word the speaker said. I just remember the sly, quick glances I'd throw over to the girls' side (in our church men and boys sat on one side of the auditorium and women and girls on the other). With each quick glance I'd focus in on a different girl and "analyze" her. Finally my gaze came to rest on one girl I'd never seen before. The glance became a stare and I forgot about checking out any other girls. I forgot about everything, until a buddy gave me a sharp poke in the ribs.

"Hey, Norm," he whispered, "you'd better pay attention to what's going on, or one of the deacons will be getting after you."

I snapped up straight in the pew and looked at the speaker. But my mind's eye was still staring at that girl. What was it about her that seemed so attractive? She wasn't beautiful—at least not by the standards of some of my friends. Her hair was sort of a very ordinary brown color, but it was tucked neatly up under her prayer covering. There was something soft and sweet and very lovely about her. She had been listening intently to the preacher and I read something intriguing in her eyes as they fastened on the visiting pastor. What was it? It was more than mere interest. It was—hunger. It was like she

4

was hanging on his every word, trying to internalize his message, drinking up every truth he spoke.

My focus drifted back to her and suddenly she glanced over at me. She was startled to see me staring at her, but her surprise quickly turned to a shy smile and then she was looking back at the speaker again, caught up in what he was saying.

That little smile told me a lot. She was shy like me, maybe even a little ashamed of herself for some reason. But inside, there lurked a spirit of fun and mischief that I felt sure I could really enjoy.

"Harold," I whispered excitedly to the boy beside me, "who's that girl, third from the aisle, two rows front? See that one with the blue dress and brown hair?"

"Oh, her. That's Betty Wenger. She's from Manheim, but she's not for you, Norm."

"Why not? Has she already got a boyfriend?" I was afraid to hear the answer, and I cringed inwardly as I waited for his reply.

"No, I don't think so. But she never goes with anyone long—says she's too busy doing things with her girlfriends. I guess she's particular or something. I really don't think you'd have much of a chance with her at all, Norm. No offense, mind you! Now, will you be quiet, please!"

With a sigh of relief I rested back in the pew. I turned my face back to the man in the pulpit and smiled. I knew who was going to be my date—Betty Wenger—and I knew she'd like me. At least I hoped so! I'd have to impress her. But no, somehow I realized already she was the kind of person who could see what you were really like inside. There'd be no use trying to put on a front. I'd just have to be myself—the thought was sort of scary. Yet, somehow I sensed I never would need to be afraid around Betty!

The service seemed to last forever and the minute the final prayer was over, all the teen-aged boys hurried outside. They always liked to position themselves just outside the church doors, in order to have a good vantage point for watching the girls file out.

I hung back timidly in the crowd of fellows. One thing, I sure didn't want to appear too anxious. But my eyes were glued to that door, When Betty finally emerged, I caught her eye again, and as it had in church, that shy, self-conscious smile lit up her face for a moment. "Why, she really is pretty!" I observed dreamily. Then she was gone with her friends, but I had no doubt about what I was going to do.

The next day right after lunch I headed over to Manheim. It was a bitterly cold, windy day in March, but I was warm and comfortable in my shiny, new 1941 Oldsmobile. It had been a gift from my father on my eighteenth birthday in payment for the years of hard work on the farm. It was also a reward for not having dated before the age of eighteen. Just driving the Olds gave me a sense of confidence that I normally lacked. Yet I was hoping Betty wouldn't notice the car. I desperately wanted her to like me for who I was, not because of the automobile I was driving. It took me about thirty minutes to drive from my family's farm in Millersville to Betty's home in Manheim and I remember that all the way over I'd get little chills of fear as I planned how I would talk to her.

When I finally reached her house I stopped the car and honked the horn. It made me chuckle to think of how the fellows went "courting" in those days. But to us, honking the horn was the proper way to do it. I didn't realize until much later the confusion I created inside the house when I stopped and honked. Betty had other sisters at home, all of whom were wondering who the lucky girl was. Evidently they did some fast arguing and finally decided to send the youngest girl, Edna, out to ask me who I wanted to see.

As she got to the car I rolled down the window and said, "Is Betty home? Could I talk to her please?"

Edna grinned delightedly and disappeared quickly back into the house. In a moment Betty appeared. She came awkwardly down the walk to the car. I knew at once that she was as nervous as I was and I almost left her standing out in the cold wind. Then I remembered my manners and invited her to get in the car so we could talk.

That's when I asked her for our first date—to go to church with me that evening. I was so nervous! I kept fiddling with my black bow tie and tilting my head to adjust the gray hat I was wearing. It must have been obvious that I was scared to death, but Betty smiled bashfully and if she noticed my uneasiness, at least didn't seem to mind it.

She accepted my invitation and ran back into the house. I don't quite remember the trip back to my home—guess I wasn't paying much attention to my driving! But I was happy, so happy that Betty Wenger would be my first date! Even milking the cows seemed easier that afternoon as I daydreamed about the special evening ahead.

That first outing together was a little difficult for both of us, but we knew right away that we were attracted to each other. Betty seemed to admire me, but I wasn't sure why. Some buddies had told me her family was rather poor—no phone or radio and a struggling little farm. This didn't concern me in the least, but I feared that maybe she liked me more for my car and reputation than for myself.

We continued to date. I discovered that Betty was not really impressed with my new car. In fact, I'm not sure she ever did know what make it was. The intangible things counted with her—kindness and gentleness shown to others, humor and quickness to forgive, the beauty in a spring flower, the music in a robin's song. She came from a very close-knit family. Each one loved and cared for the others. Her father was the kind of man who brought wildflowers to his wife when she was discouraged and prayed for each of his children by name. Her mother sang cheerfully as she worked. These were the endearing qualities that really counted with Betty.

I wanted desperately to give her all that would make her happy. I tried my best to measure up to her expectations.

Our attraction for each other grew. The night she appeared at the door with a new, navy blue coat, a soft navy-and-white dress and black patent leather slippers with tiny bows, I wished I could take her in my arms and tell her how lovely she was. She looked so sweet and vulnerable. As it was though, it took awhile till I could even muster enough courage to hold her hand. Then the sparks flew! Whatever it is that ignites the flame of physical attraction between a young man and woman happened in that moment when

I took her hand. I knew there would never be anyone else but Betty in my life.

The course of our love was not to be such an easy one, however. I was wrestling so much with my own timidity and insecurity, that I was blind to some of those same feelings in Betty. All I noticed was that she would try to make me jealous. That really wasn't a very difficult task since I desperately wanted to keep her as my girlfriend. It became apparent that she actually felt inferior to me and tried to build herself up by talking about other fellows.

Every time she hinted that someone else was interested in her, I became angry. Yet, I tried to hold my anger inside and appear calm. I was like a smoldering volcano. My cover eventually blew off and we ended up arguing.

Her home situation didn't help our relationship either. Oh, Betty's parents liked me well enough but they kept telling Betty that she wasn't good enough for me. It seemed impossible to them that I could really love Betty, poor as she was. To me, she was rich in qualities I admired—sensitivity to the needs of others, an intense desire to be of help, an appreciation for the splendor of the world around us. She had so many good qualities which drew me to her!

Then her parents would tell her I couldn't be really in love with her, since I had never dated anyone else. They were convinced I should date around a bit and get to know some other girls. Betty was insecure enough to believe them. She would declare to me that we just had to break up, yet I perceived that deep down, she really didn't want to. We would argue back and forth and the whole relationship became increasingly difficult until finally we did break up.

Those were miserable days for me! I didn't want to date any other girl. Still, I knew her parents would never be satisfied until I did.

Actually, I needed to do something to please the Wengers. I had humiliated myself at their home not long after I started dating Betty. She had invited me home to meet her folks and have a meal with the whole family… all nine of them! It was obvious that she had spent hours working to have the table set perfectly and the atmosphere conducive to a favorable impression for both me and her parents. I was nervous—I was obviously "under inspection"—but I forced myself to appear calm and collected.

All went smoothly until we sat down to eat and her father looked at me and asked simply, "Norm, would you return thanks for us before the meal?" It was a simple enough question, at least to Mr. Wenger. Betty had told me how he prayed with the family each day and how sometimes she heard him praying for his children in the early morning hours. He was a real man of God. But I had never prayed out loud in my life! Sure, I prayed quietly at home, and I know my parents also did, but no one in our family ever prayed out loud. I didn't have the faintest idea how to start. I just sat there, paralyzed with fear, a giant lump clogging my throat. Looking very red and very uncomfortable, I sat staring at the plate.

Everyone else sat there with their heads bowed, everyone except Betty, that is. She kept looking at me with pleading eyes, as if to say, "You're not making a very good impression this way!"

Desperately, I wished I could think of something to say. Inwardly I cried out, "Lord, help me!" but I couldn't speak one word. Finally, after what seemed like an hour, Mr. Wenger returned thanks and everyone dug into the food. I figured the whole family had just labeled me "a heathen." The mood of the day had been spoiled. I was afraid it would take a long time for Betty's family to get over that goof!

This had convinced Betty that I needed to learn quickly how to pray out loud. She even may have wondered how much of a Christian I really was. So, for a while, she insisted that we pray together on our dates. I liked this because I desired to know God better. Betty and I had both accepted Christ as our Savior in our early teens. It was due to her father's teaching that Betty had first realized she was a sinner in need of God's forgiveness. She had believed that the death of Jesus Christ was in substitution for her and that because of His resurrection, she could live eternally. Humbly and sincerely she asked Him to be her Savior. I had made the same decision at our church. We were sure we would go to heaven when we died. Yet neither of us felt much satisfaction with our spiritual lives. I read my Bible each day and tried to pray (silently, of course!). The Bible stories were interesting, but I never could relate them to my own life. My praying usually resulted in a kind of vague promise to a distant God that I would wear plain clothes, keep my car painted black and follow the strict codes of the Mennonite church.

Then, when Betty and I stopped dating, I wished more than ever that I could get through to God. I surely needed help, but I just didn't know how to get it.

I was proud and had told Betty stubbornly that we wouldn't get back together until she was ready. She would have to make the first move. I wouldn't come crawling back to her, although I considered it many times. When I would see her with other fellows it would tear me up. I decided I had to fight back somehow, so I began dating other girls. I tried to pick pretty and popular girls, because I knew jealousy was just as much of a problem for Betty as it was for me. Some of my friends helped me out by making certain Betty was informed when I had a date and where I went, just to make her more envious.

About two long months later, I received a card in the mail. When I noticed the Manheim postmark, my heart started thumping. Could it be? When I pulled it out of the envelope and saw the picture of the flower-filled wheelbarrow on the front of the card, I knew it had to be from Betty. She was crazy about flowers. Trembling, I opened the card and glanced down at the simple words. A lump formed in my throat and I felt like a huge burden had rolled off my back. It said simply, "To love is to remember and I love to remember you." It was as good as saying she would marry me! I would never let her get away from me again.

When we met each other at church later we felt confident the conflicts between us were gone for good. We promised our love to each other then and there and looked forward with excitement to our future. Neither of us was allowed to get married before the age of twenty-one. So we had three wonderful years of getting to know each other, longing and planning for the day when we would become husband and wife.

We set the date for November 27, 1943. With me still working on my father's farm, we had no choice but to plan our wedding for winter when farm work was lighter. It would also give us more time to set up housekeeping. My parents had promised to fix up their little tenant house for us so I could continue farming for them. To Betty and me it was like a sweet dream; we imagined ourselves keeping house in the cute little cottage and starting a family. At times, I feared things might not work out just as we had dreamed, but I tried to push such nagging doubts into the background as young lovers do.

As the day approached I grew increasingly nervous and tense. This was partly due to the fact that 1 was still a shy, quiet guy who dreaded to stand out in a crowd. And Betty, who would choke up giving a book report in school, wasn't much braver. We decided to have the smallest ceremony possible—just immediate family and then a small reception for about forty guests. "The smaller the better!" we both agreed.

My anxiety was increased by the fact that my parents just weren't doing anything to get the little tenant house ready for us. They had assured me that we could live there, but as the day for our marriage approached, nothing had been done to make it livable.

But with the optimism of youth, I came to the wedding feeling that surely things would work out fine in the end for us. We'd live on love, I figured.

Our wedding day dawned bright and sunny—an unusually beautiful day for the end of November. I was at Betty's home early to make sure everything was ready. Pacing nervously, I wondered if I would make it through the ceremony. But when Betty came into the parlor, glowing with excitement and beautiful in her white velvet dress, much of my fear left.

She had longed to carry some flowers with her, but the rules of our church would not permit brides to do this. However, she didn't need any flowers because she looked so lovely! We huddled in a corner, whispering excitedly, expecting the arrival of the preacher.

We waited and waited. The wedding ceremony was scheduled for 10:00 a.m. and when 9:45 came and went, Betty was literally shaking.

"Where is he? He should have been here long ago! If the preacher doesn't come, how can we get married?" She was on the verge of tears.

Something had to be done, so I sent one of her family to a neighbor's house, where there was a phone, to call the minister and find out what was delaying him.

When our messenger returned, his news really didn't cheer us up. The preacher had confused the wedding time and was still working in the fields. He had to get cleaned up first, but would try to make it over to Betty's house just as quickly as possible.

How could he have forgotten the time of our ceremony? Did he consider us so unimportant? Our self-respect dwindled even more.

In the meantime the guests were arriving for the reception. They expected to greet the new bride and groom. Instead, they saw a pitifully jittery pair standing in the corner. I tried my best to console Betty and assure her we really would be married that day, but as each new guest arrived and the story had to be repeated over and over, our tension grew.

Finally the preacher arrived. The parlor was in a general state of confusion. People weren't sure whether they should be witnessing this wedding or not, since they had been invited only for a reception. The room was crowded and it took some arranging to get us positioned in front of the pastor. And the poor man was so upset by his mistake that he stumbled through the ceremony as if he had never performed a wedding before.

When it was all over, people teased us about all the preacher's mistakes and questioned whether we were sure we were legally married. I knew this teasing didn't help Betty's peace of mind. But I held up the license and assured everyone that that piece of paper was what really counted anyway. "The preacher pronounced us man and wife and I'm going to act like I'm married!" I announced triumphantly.

Our honeymoon was short—two days to be exact—but it was great. My father had insisted that I be back to work on Tuesday and I knew I didn't dare disobey him, even though I was now a married man. My father was an outgoing man who could be a real gentleman. But he had a strong temper in those days and I certainly didn't want to make him angry. Besides, we were still believing he would be fixing up the tenant house at anytime, so we especially wanted to keep on his good side.

I had no doubt that Betty would be a wonderful wife. She seemed so willing to give of herself for me and it was nice to be spoiled a little for a change. I was accustomed to wearing myself out on the farm for my dad's profit, and it was a sweet and refreshing experience to have someone interested only in serving me.

Betty and I had decided we'd have to arrange temporary housing until the tenant house was ready. So, although we dreaded the separation, she resolved to return to her home following the honeymoon and I returned to mine. I would do my farm work during the week and get up to see her whenever possible. Then on weekends we would stay together.

That was the hardest parting I ever endured. As I drove Betty back to her home in Manheim, following our brief honeymoon, I was terribly discouraged. To leave my bride of only two days, and head back to the farm alone was an unbearable thought. But it seemed we had no choice. We clung tenderly to each other for a long time, before I finally could bring myself to leave her and reluctantly start back to Millersville.

By the middle of the week I could bear the separation no longer. Betty was miserable as well. I went up to see her on Wednesday evening and suggested that she come back to the farm with me. I had asked my parents if we could live in one of the rooms in their huge farmhouse, until spring when we would move into the little tenant house. They had agreed and Betty was overjoyed at the thought of being together again.

I must admit I had some hidden fears. My parents really didn't know Betty too well and I wanted desperately for them to like her a lot. My pride made me eager to prove to them that I had successfully chosen a wonderful wife, without their help. So I overdid it!

Each day, after we moved into my parents' home, I'd brag about Betty's cooking abilities and housekeeping prowess. Trouble was, this just put more pressure on her to measure up to my boasting. She felt uneasy and inferior to start with, being in this lovely, huge house, with people she had always been told were much better than her. Things went terribly!

16

She burned the cookies, ruined the fried oysters, and generally said and did the wrong thing at the wrong time. I pitied her, but just aggravated the problem by trying to defend her mistakes. Everyone was getting tense. My mother and sisters did all they could to be kind and helpful. Betty loved them for it, but she still made mistake after mistake.

Then Betty got a taste of my father's temper. She was so sensitive, so afraid inside. It was more than she could handle to be around someone who could fly into a rage so easily.

She finally begged for us to leave the farm and live somewhere else. I loved her so much and I hated seeing her hurt and afraid. It also made sense to me that time alone together would help get our marriage on firmer ground. By now, it was obvious that my folks were in no hurry to prepare our little home for us.

We left the farm and settled as tenant farmers on another farmer's property some miles away from my family. It was a difficult break with my folks and they really took it hard. We hadn't wanted to cause hard feelings, but it was beginning to look like whatever we did, problems followed us.

And problems certainly followed us there. The split from my folks was just one of many major difficulties which were to come our way.

As I sat on the milking stool that day in the barn, reminiscing about our courtship and early days of marriage, I knew I could never put Betty in an institution. Somehow we would make it. In the only way I knew how to pray, I cried out, "Lord, help us! I just don't know what to do!"

2

Trials, Trauma and Tranquilizers

As I struggled on with my work that day, it would have encouraged me to know that God really was going to bring us help soon. But at the time all I could see was the mountain of problems which had been piling on top of us.

It wasn't just Betty who was suffering. The whole family was plagued with pain and sickness. Had we known as a young couple starting out on our own, the difficulties we had in store for us, I'm sure we would have fled in terror.

How I wished Betty would try to get over her self-pity and help the rest of us who were also suffering. I guess she had faced just too much. I couldn't blame her. She'd been through more in thirteen years of marriage than most folks face in a lifetime. We had had more than our share of hardships.

Ruefully, I recalled the chain of events which had now brought us to the end of ourselves.

When we left my home after two months of marriage and began farming on our own, we figured our big problems were over. Life in the future looked so appealing.

True, we were poor. We set up housekeeping in a few rooms of an old, drafty farmhouse. We had no heat and no inside bathroom. I worked hard for two men who often seemed to be at each other's throats. Often, I would be caught in the middle as peacemaker. Our pay was eighteen dollars a week and it was a constant battle to make ends meet. Still, we were happy. We had a garden and Betty was thrilled to bring in the fresh vegetables to can for the months to come. We were learning to work together and plan for the future.

We had to plan, because just a couple of months after finally setting out on our own, Betty became pregnant. In those days, our kind old family doctor charged about fifty dollars to deliver a baby at home. Fifty dollars seemed like a fortune to me, but I was determined to save for it.

Betty and I had more than a few fights over my miserliness during those days of waiting. One night we went to the grocery store and she begged for an ice cream cone. I refused and we argued all the way home.

To make things even more difficult, Betty's doctor had told her she was eating for two, so she needn't try to control her weight. Wanting the baby to be strong and healthy, I went along with the doctor's orders, encouraging her to eat a lot (at least as much as I could afford)!

How excited we were at the thought of being parents! We would lie awake at night whispering plans and hopes for our little one. As a girl, Betty had taught herself to bake and sew, and she wasted no time during her pregnancy in making preparation for the happy event. She sewed little baby clothes and soon had a completed layette awaiting our baby. I was so proud of her—she tried to have everything so nice, even on our limited income.

We had no idea what to expect as far as the birth of the baby was concerned. Having read no books on the subject, we ignorantly planned on it being an easy experience.

Not long after Betty's labor began though, we realized it was not going to be an easy experience. We phoned the doctor and he arrived at the house quickly. I stood anxiously by Betty's side, holding her hand. Observing the worried expression on the doctor's face, my apprehension mounted. I had been hoping that soon I would be congratulated. Instead, the doctor grimly informed me that Betty was having complications and that she must be taken to the hospital immediately.

It was a bitterly cold and snowy day in January, and we lived about five miles from the hospital. The trip through the snowstorm was terrible. It was almost impossible to see through the blinding snow and the roads were hazardous. It was not possible for the doctor to drive fast and at times I wondered if I would lose both Betty and the baby on the way.

Arriving at St. Joseph's Hospital in Lancaster, Betty was rushed into a labor room in which husbands were not permitted. I found out later that she was in with five or six other women, all of whom were groaning or screaming. It terrified Betty. In many ways she still seemed like a child herself. She didn't deserve to be suffering, I thought.

A specialist was called in and I waited through the rest of the day and all night, wondering what was happening to my wife. I waited alone. I felt like I had no one to turn to. I prayed and pleaded with God, but as usual my prayers seemed powerless.

In the morning the specialist emerged with news. It was brief and discouraging. Betty had given birth to a son. He weighed almost eleven pounds and was a beautiful baby. But he had been injured at birth and was not expected to live. Betty was also in serious condition. She could die at any time.

"May I see Betty, doctor?" I asked. I had to be near her and try to comfort her, although I dreaded giving her the disheartening news.

"Yes, you can go in to see her," the doctor replied, "but don't say anything about the baby's condition. It will only worry her and that could kill her at this point. She mustn't know anything about the baby yet."

That seemed to make things even more difficult, but I went to her room quickly,

She looked pale and weak, but greeted me with a brave smile. I just held her close, telling her over and over how much I loved her and cared for her.

"Did you see him yet, Norm? We have a son! They said they would bring him to me soon. I'm sure he will be beautiful! Don't you think so too?" Betty ran out of breath and reached out her hand to clasp mine.

"Yes, I'm sure he's beautiful. Our dear little Jay Kenneth Charles. I'm proud of you, Betty, and I love you so much. How are you feeling?"

21

"Tired and weak—and very sore, but just you wait, I'll be back up and around in no time. Why didn't anyone ever tell me it was so hard to have a baby?" She laughed, but the tears trickling down her cheeks betrayed her pain. "Anyway, it was worth it," she continued proudly, "and I can't wait to hold little Kenneth. Norm, when you leave will you ask the nurse to bring me the baby soon?"

"Sure I will and I can't stay here long anyway. The doctor told me you need lots of rest. You've had a long hard night. Goodbye, sweetheart." I bent over to kiss her and felt the cold sweat on her forehead. It chilled me as the doctor's words raced through my mind again. "It just couldn't be—it wouldn't happen," I argued with myself. But as I turned to go, a little shiver ran through my body and I wished time could just stand still for a while. I was terrified of what the future might bring.

The nursery was just down the hall and I hurried there to see the baby. The nurse pointed him out to me and I gazed at the most lovely baby I had ever seen. He was long and plump and had beautiful, thick black hair. He certainly looked healthy, I thought.

I motioned for the nurse and she came over to speak with me.

"The doctor said our little Kenneth isn't expected to live. But I don't understand. What's wrong with him?"

"I don't know the extent of his injuries, Mr. Charles. I know he has a broken arm and there are several marks on his forehead from the difficult birth procedures. I believe these may have caused brain damage. I'm so sorry, Mr. Charles."

I was silent for a moment and she turned to leave. "Wait, Nurse, my wife wants very badly to see the baby. Couldn't you take him in to her soon?"

"I'll check with the doctor, but I'm sure it will be okay. Although she won't be allowed to hold the baby. Your wife is much too weak right now to hold an eleven-pound baby, and the baby shouldn't be handled any more than necessary either."

There wasn't much more I could do, so I decided to return home. Alone and dejected, I had to trudge the five miles back to our house because no public transportation was available, due to the snowstorm. I was shivering from the cold and the icy fear which was chilling my heart. The world looked bleak.

When I returned the next morning, I was greeted by a solemn-faced doctor. Fear wrapped itself around my heart and squeezed tight. I prepared myself for bad news.

Our little Kenny had just died. They had tried their best to save him, but their efforts were in vain. And what's more, Betty was struggling for her life. If she could survive the next three days, she'd probably recover, but he held out little hope for her to last through even one more day. For certain she must not be told about the baby's death or the shock would kill her.

What I had dreaded had happened. I could hardly believe it was true, yet I had no choice but to face up to the fact. There was nothing to do but accept it and go on with living. Although the living could never be the same, I thought. I notified Betty's family right away and called my parents too. Everyone expressed their sorrow and sympathy, yet they couldn't possibly understand the misery and loneliness I was feeling.

It's amazing I even survived the next week without suffering a nervous breakdown myself. There were arrangements to make for the baby's funeral, which I would have to attend by myself. Betty still was not to know about little Kenneth's death. There were trips to the hospital to visit Betty. She seemed no better and it was agonizing to skirt her constant questions about the baby's welfare. There were preparations to be made in light of Betty's probable death. By then I held out little hope for her recovery.

It was following the baby's funeral that I arrived at the hospital to find Betty frantic and hysterical. It seems that an uncaring nurse, angered by Betty's attempts to get out of bed, had lashed out unkindly, "Just you watch, Mrs. Charles. If you don't stay in bed like you're supposed to, you're going to wind up dead just like your baby!"

What a way for her to have to discover the truth! I did everything I could to calm and console her, but she was distraught. I really couldn't blame her. Yet the more she sobbed, the more I feared for her life. One thing I knew, I wanted desperately for Betty to live. I just couldn't face losing her.

Once in a while our minister had mentioned divine healing. I didn't know much about it, although I seemed to recall something about the elders of the church laying hands on the sick and anointing them with oil for healing. It appeared to be our only chance—the last straw. I suggested the idea to Betty.

She seemed almost to have given up on life after she found out about the baby's death. She did not seem to particularly like the idea of prayer for her healing. In fact, she confided to me that she had already confessed a lot of her sins to God. She wanted to die with a "clean slate." I never doubted

24

that Betty loved me, but it made me feel utterly abandoned to hear her talk about her own death. I know she caught a glimpse of the terror I had of being left alone. And maybe that's what changed her mind. At any rate, she finally consented to call for the bishop and deacon of the church.

My spirit lifted to think that these men of God were going to pray for my Betty. I always looked up to the church leaders as being on very good terms with God. I envied them. For the first time in several days of misery, I began to have some hope. But when they arrived in the hospital room, they gave us a lecture on the will of God. They pointed out all too clearly that it might not be God's will to heal her. I couldn't understand why God would want my young wife to die, but I was also afraid to question any minister's word. To me they were like the voice of God. I began to wonder if God even wanted to hear our prayer.

Betty had been raised a Mennonite and she obeyed the church rules outwardly, but I knew that inside she carried a hard spirit of rebellion. She was forever trying to put a flower on her dress, or hide the strings of her prayer covering, wear lighter-colored stockings, or a brighter dress. Nonetheless, she was a Christian and it had been Betty who had challenged me repeatedly about my relationship to Christ. She was the one who first coaxed me to pray out loud. She was the one who told me of her longing to know the Jesus who had moved so miraculously in the New Testament. She was the one who had persuaded me to pray as a young husband, "Lord, bring anything into our lives to bring us closer to you." But if living up to the standards of the church was what mattered most to God (and I feared it was), I wasn't sure Betty would merit God's special attention.

25

When they finally got around to praying for her, my hopes had waned again.

Soon after we prayed, I phoned my sister-in-law, asking her to have Betty's wedding dress cleaned. She had said she wanted to be buried in it! That shows what little faith we had! It seemed I might as well continue making funeral preparations. If God was more concerned with Betty's appearance than her inner faith (as I suspected), and if He might not even want her to live anyway (which the ministers implied), I reasoned that there wasn't much chance of a healing.

I guess God wanted to prove me wrong though and those men of God probably had a lot more faith than I had given them credit for—because Betty got well! I was surprised and very, very happy!

About two weeks later she came home from the hospital. It was disheartening to come home without the baby we had looked forward to so much. And it was hard to acknowledge the staggering financial debts we now faced. The fifty dollars I had so carefully saved had been used up the first night in the hospital. Still, in my heart was an overflowing thankfulness to God for Betty's recovery.

As soon as the doctor permitted, we started plans for a family again. When Betty became pregnant this time we watched her weight carefully. The specialist at the hospital had discovered that Betty had a deformed pelvis. This had caused the difficulty with delivering such a large baby as Kenny. So this time she must have a smaller baby.

Our daughter, Joann, was born in December, 1946. She weighed six and one quarter pounds and was fine. It had been a difficult delivery again and when it was all over the doctor informed us that any other babies we planned on having would have to be delivered by Caesarean section. He told us it was a miracle that our little girl hadn't suffered brain damage from the high forceps they were forced to use in her delivery. We were just so thankful for our baby girl that we didn't worry much about the future. Our center of attention was little Joann! For a while nothing else mattered much.

Not long after bringing Joann home, Betty began smocking dresses and sewing fancy coats and bonnets for our daughter. It seemed that Betty wanted to put all the adornments on the baby that she herself had been forbidden, by the church, to use. I accused her often of harboring the sin of pride, but she would argue that it was just "motherly love." She was still nervous and insecure and most suggestions I made were rejected with a defensive spirit. We usually ended up arguing.

Nevertheless I was proud of Joann too and loved to take care of her. I sincerely wanted to help Betty, because her health never seemed to be very good. But I also found so much joy and satisfaction in caring for a little one. So much of my life I had felt rather unwanted and unnecessary, but this tiny being loved me and depended on me. Now there were two people who needed me—Betty and little Joann. It was good to feel needed.

The next few years seemed to fly by. It was as if we were always moving, going to the doctor, or preparing for another baby. My father began visiting us more frequently and it surprised us when he shared that he would be retiring from the farm. He was buying a house in town and wanted us to move into the big farmhouse to take over the farm work for him. We were thrilled! The farm was beautiful—a perfect place to raise a family. It had a large meadow and garden and a meandering stream. It was a child's paradise. We felt immense excitement as we moved into the spacious, attractive house with our growing family. We began adjusting to the work pattern again. It was a challenge for me to take on such a responsibility. I felt proud that my dad had entrusted it to me.

In spite of the joy of living on the farm, Betty got sick pretty often. At least she thought she was sick. One day she announced her certainty that she had tuberculosis and insisted that I take her for a chest X-ray; some time later it was a "serious heart condition" that "required an electrocardiogram." Then it was cancer and another trip to a specialist. Of course all these tests proved negative. I was beginning to wonder where this imagination of hers was going to lead. Yet whenever I would try to correct her gently, or suggest that she work on getting these "fool notions" out of her head, we would end up in an argument. Sometimes she would refuse to speak to me for a day or so.

One night after such an argument, she was feeling especially sorry for herself. So, just to worry me, she hid in the closet, thinking I would search frantically for her. When I fell asleep without so much as calling her, she was really upset. The atmosphere was tense and uncomfortable. But then the storm passed. We made up and things glided along fine—until the next time.

Two years after Joann was born, Betty gave birth to Jim. Two years later, our son John came along. After another two years, our twins, Marvin and Mervin, were born. The doctor advised us to stop having children, because Betty wouldn't be able to survive another C-section. The twins' births had been touch-and-go as it was.

We were satisfied with our family of five children. Each child was so different, yet so special to us. We were thrilled with each new baby. Life settled into something of a routine. It soon became apparent however, that "routine" for us meant a running streak of accidents and illnesses.

For example, there was the day I heard a blood-curdling scream from the direction of the house. I left the barn on the double and was horrified to look up and see four-year-old Joann hanging from the gatepost with a large hook protruding through her cheek. The doctor stitched her up, but he warned us that the puncture may have damaged her saliva gland. This could have disfigured her face permanently. Mercifully however, the hook had narrowly missed the gland and she retained only a small scar from the accident.

Then there was the day we entertained several relatives. It was a scorching summer afternoon and we decided to treat the children to giant-sized ice cream cones. Not long after the party, our little Jim ran screaming to the kitchen. His face was scarlet and he was choking. He had found a glass of turpentine out by the workshop and had gulped down the whole thing. We called the doctor who arrived shortly to take us to the hospital. Speeding into town at ninety miles an hour, he kept urging us to keep Jim awake.

The doctors pumped his stomach. They believed Jim's mouth and throat were burned and that he might not eat for a few days. However, the ice cream he had eaten just before the accident had coated his stomach and protected it from being badly burned by the turpentine. We were filled with gratitude that Jim was alive. As soon as we entered the kitchen upon arriving back at the farm, we were surprised to see Jim rush over to the cupboard and beg for some soda crackers. Betty and I were ecstatic with joy and relief, although still rather shaken and guilt-ridden for not keeping a closer eye on our mischievous son.

The worst accident, however, happened to me in the autumn of 1952. I had gone to my brother-in-law's farm to help cut corn and haul it to his silo. By 1:45 a.m. we had done a lot of work, but the chopper which blew the corn to the top of the silo had become choked and work had stopped. I decided to climb up the silo to see how full it was. At lunch time, it was always fun to brag about how much work we had finished and it was also important to know how hard we would have to work in the afternoon to complete our tasks.

So I proceeded to climb the silo. When I reached a height of about thirty-six feet I realized I was just above the top of the silage. I was pleased with the morning's accomplishment. The other workers would be glad to hear my report.

But my feelings of self-satisfaction did not continue for long. The spot on which I was standing was actually a rung on one of the numerous doors which ran up the side of the silo. What I didn't know was that there was a defective hook on that particular door. Understandably, with the weight of my body resting on it, it gave out!

The door swung inward, carrying my feet along. The sudden jolt made me lose my grip and there was nothing to grab within reach. My hands pawed frantically at the air. I squeezed my eyes shut, hoping to block out the terrifying glimpse of my deathbed thirty-six feet below. Down I fell, headfirst onto the concrete floor!

I instinctively put my arm over my head for protection. Therefore, it received the brunt of the crash. I can remember gasping for breath, feeling as though my lungs would explode and finally sensing that welcome air seeping slowly back into my chest.

We realized later I must have lain there unconscious for fifteen minutes or so. The other men were working on the opposite side of the silo and were completely unaware that anything had happened to me.

When I finally came to, I stumbled groggily around to the front of the barn. I was greeted by incredulous stares from the others. Then my brother-in-law's expression changed to one of horror as he guessed what must have happened to me.

"Bob, get your pick-up over here fast and take Norm to the doctor!" he shouted at one of the other workers. "Hurry up, man! He's in bad shape!"

I certainly looked a mess and felt much worse! My arm was hanging like jelly by my side. I was so dizzy I could barely walk straight. My dirty work clothes were even dirtier from the silage that had continued falling on me as I had lain unconscious at the base of the silo.

My friend, Bob, who drove me into town, kept poking me to keep me from fainting. Somehow I managed to direct him to Dr. Rigano's office.

When I hobbled in, the doctor himself was the first person to greet us. He stared in amazement and then said, "What on earth happened to you?"

I started to explain, but before I could finish one sentence, he interrupted. "Never mind the details now. You've got to get to the hospital right away. You can give me the rest of the story later."

So we were back in Bob's truck, racing to the hospital. A policeman even let us run a red light when he took one look at me. I must have looked like death itself.

The hospital ordeal was in some ways worse than the accident. After being ordered from department to department, only to find doctors out for lunch, or technicians unavailable, I couldn't keep up with the pace any longer. Everything swayed in front of me and I went down—in the middle of the dispensary floor.

Consciousness came and went several times during the next hours. Once I heard a doctor's distant voice asking incredulously, "Do I really understand what a silo is? If it's what I think it is and this guy fell from one and is alive to tell about it—I don't believe it—I just don't believe it!"

Another time I realized there were several medical people in the room with me. A couple of them were cutting my shirt off. Evidently my arm had swelled to such a size that there was no other way to remove it. Everything seemed very hazy and far away. Someone in the room mentioned that I was turning gray and the end was "not far away now."

"Ridiculous," I thought to myself. "I haven't given up yet. I'm not going to die." I determined to get well.

And I did recover—at least to some degree. I had suffered a severe concussion, my arm was broken in four places, my wrist was crushed and my back was injured as well. After a few days, the doctors concluded the concussion had caused no serious problems. They released me to go home. I wore a cast for weeks on my arm and it healed. I went to therapy several times a week for months to regain use of my wrist. However, the bones knit incorrectly, so reluctantly I returned to the hospital to have them broken again and reset. Then after much more therapy, I finally regained normal use of my wrist.

However, my back did not heal. The doctors suggested all sorts of treatments and I was willing to try anything. Nothing worked! I returned to farm work in pain. I was beginning to dread the future.

As I would pull myself out of bed in the morning I would grit my teeth and sometimes fall on my knees to keep from crying out in pain. People had always thought of me as a "real man"—one who would never flinch a muscle if hurt. What would they have thought if they could have seen me then, agonizing over every move? It would have been like heaven to have stayed in bed and rested, but I had to keep on with the farm work. By this time we had accumulated so many medical bills that I dared not miss a day of work. More and more frequently my stomach ulcer flared up as well. This had developed around the time of the death of our first baby. From that time on, whenever I got nervous or upset, I'd break out in a cold sweat, vomit and sometimes pass out.

I felt that surely nothing more could go wrong. Yet I feared that with our record it surely would.

I was right in my fears. In the fall of 1954, Joann was scheduled to enter the hospital for a routine tonsillectomy. Just before the operation they were running normal tests and a urinalysis revealed that she had chronic nephritis, a disease of the kidney. Her kidney was permanently damaged. There was little we could do but watch Joann endure weakness and discomfort. Relentlessly, this silent killer plagued her, causing her to miss a year of school.

Next it was John. He came down with rheumatic fever. In those days this often resulted in severe complications. For him, it brought a serious heart murmur. The doctor ordered him to be admitted to Heart Haven Hospital.

Betty couldn't face the prospect of little Johnny being left alone in the hospital. He was a very sensitive child and we were sure the separation would hinder, rather than hasten, his recovery. So Betty begged to let him stay at home. The doctor finally relented, with the stipulation that he remain in a rented hospital bed at all times. He was not to get out, even to use the bathroom. Our little boy who had loved running and playing on the farm was now bedfast. And there was little hope that he would be able to get out of bed for a long time.

By this time Betty was surviving from day to day on anxiety medications. I pitied her—she just couldn't cope with all our problems. Purchasing her expensive pills only contributed more to our financial burdens and instead of becoming calmer, Betty became increasingly nervous and despondent.

We frequently cried out to God to help us. More than once I had fallen on my knees out behind the barn and begged God to do something. Why was He letting all this happen to us?

Our church friends warned us never to question God, but we couldn't suppress the big "Why?" that was always foremost in our minds. Someone told me God must surely have something special in store for me, or He wouldn't have preserved us through all these calamities. That was one way of looking at it. Although if He loved us so much, I reasoned He could have spared us from the problems in the first place. Someone quoted the verse, "Whom the Lord loves, He chastens" (Heb. 12:6). Well, in that case we concluded we must be His special "pets!"

I was in turmoil, in pain, in debt and afraid. If God really loved me so much surely He would do something soon. He had to, because I was sure I couldn't go on much longer!

Each day continued more or less the same for months. We tried everything to help our ailing family—osteopaths, medical doctors, chiropractors, natural foods, vegetable juices, vitamins, rare brands of tea. We latched onto any new remedy like drowning seamen. Our medicine chest was full, our basement was crammed with various health contraptions. More bills—but no help! With each failure and disappointment I'd cry out again to God.

Perhaps from mere repetition and frequency of begging for help, I was beginning to feel like maybe He really was hearing me. In fact, it was almost as if I was starting to hear Him too.

For months I'd wrestled with my conscience about the fact that I had to farm tobacco. To my family it was unthinkable that anyone could run a successful farm without raising tobacco.

I had never smoked, and I had never thought much about the moral implications of raising something to be used for a habit I could not condone. At least I had not thought much about it, until things began to get so desperate for us and I started calling on God more often. Each day I just felt more and more guilty about what I was doing. It was like God was saying, "You want me to help you, yet you're not willing to obey me. You must learn to obey!"

It wasn't easy to announce my decision to quit farming tobacco. But from the moment I made up my mind and promised God I wouldn't plant another tobacco crop, I had some flickers of peace in my spirit. It was a strange and welcome feeling.

As I finished up my farm work that day, I wondered if Betty would still be hiding in bed when I went in the house. I would have to quit my daydreaming and get back to the problems of the moment. My back was aching terribly and the babysitter had just left for home. I could envision my ailing children in their beds and the active twins brewing up some mischief. Even so, my heart felt a little lighter than usual because I had almost finished bringing in the last of the tobacco harvest. And it would be my last tobacco harvest. Seemed like my burden of guilt was getting lighter as I neared this goal.

And I was more certain than ever that I wouldn't put Betty in that institution. How could I add that guilt to my burden now? So far, we had been through everything together. I couldn't bear to change that. We simply would have to make it somehow. Maybe giving up tobacco had proved to God that I meant business, that I really wanted to obey Him. God would help us—maybe. How I prayed that He would! I gave our family's pet cow, Jane, a light rap and with a sigh turned toward the house for supper. Things couldn't get any worse, could they?

3

A New Wife—A New Life

Our farm kitchen was large and bright. Somehow it always cheered me a bit to enter that room. It was usually filled with the tempting smells, busy carryings-on by the children and that comfortable atmosphere that communicated "home" to me.

That evening I entered rather warily, wondering what to expect. Would Betty still be hiding from her problems at the bottom of our bed? At first glance, all seemed calm enough. I was pleasantly surprised to see Betty dressed neatly and moving about the stove preparing supper. The aroma of the meat loaf in the oven soothed my nerves. I knew the doctor must have been wrong about her. She didn't need to be committed to any mental hospital. Surely this phase she was going through was already starting to pass.

Joann and Johnny were in their beds in the big room off the kitchen. I went in to give them both a hug and ask them how their day had been. "How interesting could it possibly be to lie there all day, looking at books, or coloring?" I reflected sadly. They seemed cheerful though, and I couldn't call them complainers.

Jim was entertaining the twins in the kitchen. Somehow he had managed to spellbind them with some of his toy horses. Blessed quietness! Outwardly all seemed to be at peace.

I crossed over and gave Betty a quick hug and kiss. I could feel the pent-up tension in her body, but I was grateful for her attempt to hide it and carry on with her responsibilities.

I disappeared into the next room to get washed up for supper. In a moment the twins started to howl. "Whatever's happened now?" I breathed to myself. Then I heard Betty's scream!

"Oh, no," I thought, "here we go again." I tore out to the kitchen, water dripping and towel still hanging over my arm.

Betty was standing immobile at the stove. In front of her the pudding she had been preparing was pouring over the edge of the kettle and flooding the stove top. For most people it would have been a minor incident—a simple case of spilled milk—nothing to cry about.

But for Betty it was the last straw. She was already convinced of her inferiority and now when she was trying her best to do something useful for a change, it turned out disastrously.

"That's it, Norm! I've had it!" she shrieked. "I just can't take it anymore. I'm leaving!" With a heart-rending sob, she threw the wooden spoon to the floor and fled out the back door.

How short-lived that reign of peace had been! By now the children were crying and calling for Betty.

"Well, I'll let Betty go now," I reasoned. "No use to chase after her till she calms down a bit anyway. And besides, the children need me more now." I got down to the difficult task of calming five scared children, cleaning up a horribly messy stove and getting what remained of supper on the table.

When supper was over and Betty still hadn't returned I began to worry. I had grown accustomed to her outbursts of temper and threats to run away. Yet I figured that inside she was much too scared and dependent to follow through on her threats. But this time, she had been gone for a long time.

I assigned the task of doing the dishes to Jim and Joann. Joann was allowed out of bed some and I figured that drying a few dishes couldn't hurt her much. However, the twins required the kind of supervision that Jim and Joann couldn't give while they were working.

So I packed Mervin under one arm and Marvin under the other and started off down the lane to hunt my wife. We checked the most obvious hiding places on the farm. But I couldn't find her. It would have been impossible to check the entire farm. It was just too large. I made one last trip down to the end of the lane. Gazing out across the meadow, I shuddered to think of Betty hiding alone out there somewhere. The September sun was dropping quickly now and the chilly night air was beginning to settle down over the fields. I hugged the twins a little tighter to me and headed dejectedly back to the house.

Somehow I managed to settle the children in bed that evening. It was difficult to calm their little spirits and assure them that mommy would be back soon. I struggled to believe my own words and quiet the doubts in my own mind. The uncomfortable lump in my throat was growing.

When the last child had finally dropped off to sleep, I flopped down in the living room to consider what my next course of action should be.

"Lord," I prayed, "I keep calling out to you to help us and so far things have been getting worse instead of better. Please Father, we're your children—we need you. We can't go on by ourselves. Please help us! We'll do whatever you want us to do, Lord, but show us what that is—because we just don't know!"

I heard the screen door in the kitchen squeak shut. It was Betty. I braced myself for the tirade of criticism and complaining which usually accompanied her "reentries." This time, though, it was surprising to watch her come meekly over to the sofa and sit down quietly beside me.

"I hunted for you, Betty," I began rather firmly. Then more gently, "The children were worried about you—and so was I."

"I know you came after me. I was hiding behind a tree in the meadow and I saw you going down the lane with the twins. I almost called out to you, but I just had to do some more thinking."

"Yeah, I know what you mean. I did a lot of thinking in the barn today. I remembered a lot about our dating days and all the hard times we've been through in the last thirteen years. I did some praying too, Betty."

"Did you really?" Her bashful little smile crept over her face for a moment. "That's what I was doing in the meadow today too—praying I mean."

"You want to tell me about it?" I prodded. Betty seemed so subdued. I was curious about what had caused this change in her attitude.

"Well, when I collapsed behind that tree I really wished I could die and escape all the misery in our home. Norm, I know I've made lots of threats before, but today I meant it! So many of our friends have told us that God must be disciplining us for something wrong in our lives and that's why nothing ever goes right for us. But I honestly couldn't figure out what was bothering Him.

"After all, when we discipline the children we at least tell them what they did wrong. It would be cruel of us to punish them without them having any idea why. Well, I figured if God loves us like He's supposed to, then why shouldn't He let us know the reason for the chastening?"

"Hey, Betty, you had better be careful," I interrupted nervously. "You know God's ways are not our ways and we shouldn't question His will."

She gave an impatient shrug. "Oh, there you go sounding like everybody else at church, Well, I'm sorry if it was the wrong thing to do (although I don't really think it was wrong), but I questioned God today. I said, 'God, if you are disciplining me, please tell me why. I want to know why!' And I can't explain it, but I heard the Lord speak clearly to me then."

"Uh—oh," I thought to myself, "the pressure is making her start to imagine things." Aloud, I responded, "You heard God's voice—out loud?"

"No, nothing like that! It wasn't an audible voice. It was—well—like a quiet voice inside me."

"What did He say to you?" I remembered the voice I had heard about the tobacco farming. Excitement mounted in me, in spite of my doubts.

"He said, 'Betty, you may have me as your Savior, but you never gave me first place in your life. I WANT FIRST PLACE IN YOUR LIFE!' I asked, 'What's keeping me from putting you first?' Then I got an eye-opener! Norm, He showed me that my selfishness and stubbornness were keeping me from putting Him first. You know I've never been one to hanker after a lot of possessions for myself. I've always felt I tried to be pretty helpful to others too, but that's not what God meant by selfishness. He showed me that I've been mostly interested in doing what I wanted to do, when I wanted to do it. And He showed me that I care too much about what other people say or think about me."

Well, that analysis seemed pretty accurate to me. I knew Betty rebelled bitterly against the church rules, yet she was so careful to put on a front so people would think she was as pious as the rest. And the family was often at the mercy of her whims—like today when she had decided to stay in bed again instead of tending to the family like she should have. Stubbornness and selfishness, huh? Maybe God really did speak to her, because the diagnosis seemed to hit the nail on the head. Could God really be starting to answer our prayers? I was anxious to hear the rest of her story.

"So what happened then, Betty?"

"I prayed and told the Lord I was really desperate for peace in my life. I said, 'I don't care if I have one friend left, I want you first in my life.' The problem is, I'm not really sure how to do that, Norm. I want God first, but I'm not sure how to go about it. I feel some better, but what about tomorrow? Our problems will still be here. I'm still frustrated. It's like I know my problem and I know the solution, but how to make it become real—I just don't know." Her voice broke.

"I wish I could help you out on that," I offered weakly. "Guess we'll just have to keep on trying to do our best and live good, honest lives. Seems that would prove to God that we want Him to be first." As I said it, I sensed the futility of my own words. We had been doing exactly that for years and look where it had got us. My heart echoed Betty's frustration.

"Let's go to bed now, it's been a big day and tomorrow is church. We need to get some rest, Betty. Maybe tomorrow will be better."

The next day dawned beautifully. It was one of those brisk autumn days when you feel overwhelmed by the beauty of nature—the kind of September Sunday when you just feel like driving real slow to Sunday school with all the windows of the car rolled down so you can drink in the fresh fall air and all the breathtaking scenery.

Joann and Johnny had been left at home with a sitter. Betty and I had managed to get Jim and the twins ready in plenty of time so we wouldn't have to rush to church.

All the way there, the events of the preceding day kept parading through my mind. "God made such a glorious world for us to live in," I mused. "Surely He could do something about giving us a little bit of joy in living!"

Betty had been quiet most of the morning. I was relieved that she had decided to make the effort to come to church, although I had winced with inward pain as I watched her down the medication which she depended on to give her strength to endure each day.

My back was especially painful, but the loveliness all around helped ease it a bit. I dreaded sitting stiffly through a long church service on those hard wooden pews. I hoped the visiting speaker that day would be unusually interesting; that would make the discomfort a little more bearable.

We attended Millersville Mennonite Church and as was the custom, the women sat on one side of the church and the men on the other. I glanced over at Betty several times during the service. She had that same look of spiritual hunger on her face that I remembered her having as a teen-ager. Except now there was a deep sorrow in her eyes which had not been there years ago. It was like the look you would imagine seeing in the eyes of drowning persons as they sought in vain for someone to rescue them. There was hopelessness and desperate desire in her eyes.

"Hang in there," I whispered to her silently. "Who knows, maybe today God will do something special for you." I turned my attention back to the speaker. He was talking enthusiastically about faith. That was a bit of a change for us. To me it seemed like our sermons were generally about rules rather than a relationship with God. Could I ever have sufficient faith to hear God speaking as clearly to me as Betty had claimed last night? Probably not, yet I longed for it with all my heart!

Every once in a while I thought I heard someone in the congregation saying something during the sermon. "No, that's impossible," I concluded. In our church everything was done "decently and in order." And for our congregation, that meant silence—dead silence. Even so, incredibly, it sounded like someone was muttering a quiet, "Amen" and now and then a "Praise the Lord." "Couldn't be," I persuaded myself again. "Besides, if someone is saying anything like that they ought to be asked to stop." The thought that anyone in the congregation might be actively involved in the message was rather unnerving. Only preachers should say spiritual things like that. It made me wish the speaker would finish up quickly so I could get out of there.

It didn't take me long to make it to the car after the service. I had rounded up the boys in no time, hoping Betty wouldn't get involved talking to people. She usually seemed worse after talking to folks at church. She was so easily hurt by what people said or didn't say. Someone always had a new "cure" to suggest for us. Well, I simply could not afford (emotionally or financially) any more sure cures!

Betty took a long time in returning to the car. As the minutes passed I became increasingly impatient and worried. When she finally came running and plopped breathlessly into the front seat, my fears were confirmed.

"Norm, now I know what we need!" she announced triumphantly.

"Oh, great! Just as I thought!" I sighed wearily, "And what is it we need this time? I thought we had tried everything already!"

"Norm, we need the baptism in the Holy Spirit!" It was a dramatic announcement and totally unexpected.

"Hey, hold it a minute, Betty. You'd better be careful! That might be a false doctrine, you know!" Actually I did not have the slightest idea what the term "baptism in the Holy Spirit" meant. It had never been talked about at my church and I was suspicious of anything that wasn't endorsed by our congregation.

"But, Honey, how could it be a false doctrine?" Betty argued. "It was Lois Ebersole who told me about it and she said that since receiving this experience, she has had more patience with her husband and children—more love and peace in her home. How could that be a false doctrine? It sounds like what I need!"

"I don't know. It sounds sort of questionable to me. You better watch out or you'll be getting into bigger trouble than ever!" I tried to muster all the authority I could in that statement. I just didn't know what to think about a spiritual solution to our problems. It scared me even to think about it and I knew I did not want Betty to talk about it anymore.

She must have noticed the tone in my voice because she suddenly clammed up and the rest of the ride home was uncomfortably silent. Neither of us said anything, but we were both doing lots of very serious thinking.

Betty was withdrawn and subdued for the rest of the day. I knew what she was thinking. She was angry at me for not being enthusiastic about her suggestion. It was her old silent treatment, her let-the-dear-man-be attitude. I tried not to let it bother me and was really glad when Monday rolled around and I was able to go back to work. At least I wouldn't have to look into her accusing eyes so often.

I told myself that this thing about the Holy Spirit was just another one of Betty's fantastic ideas. Probably if we got involved in anything like that, we would be branded as heretics—plus whatever we tried usually ended up costing us money. I couldn't afford any more wild schemes.

About the middle of that week I returned from the fields to discover one of the biggest surprises of my life. I was late finishing up work and without fail that always made Betty furious with me. I was getting psyched up for the onslaught of complaining which would be awaiting me.

Instead, as I walked cautiously through the door, I was greeted with a cheery "Hi, Sweetie," from Betty. Before I could utter a sound, she had continued. "Norm, I went ahead and gave the children supper. I hope you don't mind. I thought I'd wait and eat with you. You must be really tired after a long day like today. Just go and wash up and I'll have our meal on the table in a minute—oh, and Norm—I love you!"

"Yeah—I—love you too," I stammered in a daze. While washing up I tried to figure out what had happened to my wife. Then it dawned on me. She was buttering me up for something. Probably had some new sure-fire cure, or was wanting some new clothes. She knew how tight I was getting with money these days—she must be softening me up for the "kill."

All evening I waited for her to swing the conversation over to her request. But it never happened. In fact, the only thing she did ask me was if I would forgive her for all the times she had hurt and wronged me. She was just as sweet as could be all evening—like a completely different person. No, she was still Betty, but not the one I'd become accustomed to lately. It was as if all her good qualities had blossomed and her temper and selfishness had faded. I really was stumped.

When we went to bed that evening, Betty put her arm around me and whispered again, "I love you, Norm!"

I waited. "It won't take long until she starts in with her nagging little criticisms," I thought. I waited some more. Nothing! No criticism, no complaining, no begging for something new—just peacefulness—sweet peace. "Tomorrow I'll get to the bottom of this," I concluded. Then I fell asleep.

Tomorrow came and went. Betty was just as sweet and helpful as on the previous day. It was making me so curious I could hardly stand it. I guess I should have asked her right away what had changed her. But I was so scared that it was some sort of an act that would end, once I caught on. And I sure didn't want it to end!

After the same kind of treatment kept on for a couple more days, I could not stand the suspense any longer. Once the children were in bed, I ushered Betty into the living room and sat her down on the sofa beside me.

"Betty, I don't know what has happened to you in the last few days. You're so different—and I want to know why! Will you tell me?"

"Of course I will," she answered excitedly. "I've been eager to tell you ever since it happened, but I decided to wait until you really wanted to hear about it. Plus, I wanted to see for myself that the change was permanent. I have no doubt now. I really am like a brand-new person! It all started on Sunday when I talked to Lois Ebersole after church."

"Uh-oh!" My defenses shot up. "Betty, I thought I warned you—"

"Now just wait a minute please and let me tell you the whole story. Do you want to know what changed me or not?"

"Yeah, I guess I really do," I replied hesitantly. Then more confidently, "Yes, I really do, Betty. Tell me what happened!"

"Well, when I was sitting in church on Sunday I could hear this person behind me saying little phrases under her breath all through the sermon—things like "Amen" and "Praise the Lord" and even "Hallelujah." I was shocked, really horrified, to hear someone saying such things in church. But still it got my curiosity up. As soon as the service ended I turned around to see who had been doing all the talking. It was Lois Ebersole."

"Who on earth is Lois Ebersole?" I asked a little sharply.

"I don't think you ever met her. I knew her when we were just girls. Actually I wasn't real friendly to her in those days, because she always seemed—well, too good for me. You know my problem with inferiority."

I nodded. How well I knew about that!

"So anyway, when I saw who it was I said, 'Why, Lois Ebersole, I haven't seen you in ages. How are you?' Well, did I get an earful. She kept saying, 'the Lord has done this and the Lord has done that!' She was just so excited about her life and she actually seemed to glow while she talked. I certainly didn't remember her to be such a radiant person.

"You know I can be pretty blunt and I blurted out, 'What in the world happened to you? You are so different from what you used to be. What changed you?'

49

"That's when she told me she had been baptized. 'So what?' I thought, 'I've been baptized too'—and then what she was talking about dawned on me. Norm, I don't know how I knew it, because we've certainly never heard the expression mentioned in our church but it suddenly popped into my head. I asked her, 'You mean you were baptized in the Holy Spirit?' She nodded.

"Norm, if she would have decided to leave at that moment I would have grabbed onto her and hung on for dear life. I felt—well, just like a drowning person reaching out for help. I was sure—sure as ever that here was the answer I needed.

"So I didn't waste any time. 'Lois,' I pleaded, 'tell me, how did you receive it? I really want to know!'

"Then she told me and it was simple—so simple! She said I should just pray and tell the Lord I was willing to put Him first in my life. Then I should just ask Him to fill me completely with His Holy Spirit. She said I didn't have to do anything but that and then just believe He had done it!

"About that time, her husband, Lester, came up to us. I had never met him before, but he had the same glowing smile that Lois had. She introduced me to Lester and then said, 'Darling, Betty's hungry too!'

" 'Well,' I thought, 'did she hear my stomach growling in church? Then I understood what she meant. I had never heard that expression before, but it sure did fit me. I was hungry, desperately hungry, for peace in my life.

"Well, you know the rest of what Sunday was like. When you weren't too enthusiastic about the idea, I decided I would leave you to your stubborn self and investigate this thing by myself. Then if it worked, maybe you would believe it too.

"I thought over what Lois had said for a day or so. I read whatever I could find about the baptism of the Holy Spirit—in the Bible—and I found an article about it too. The author said that when we're saved we do have the Holy Spirit, but the big question is, 'Does He have all of us?' I prayed a lot and finally I was sure of what I had to do. So I went into the bedroom. First, I simply asked the Lord to show me if there were some things that I needed to make right with people. The Lord really is fair with us, isn't He? If He would have made me confess all the wrongs I've committed in my life, I guess I'd be going to people yet. But He showed me only about six people whom I needed to go to, to make things right. You were one of them, Norm.

"Anyway, I simply promised the Lord I would take care of this responsibility. I'm sure He knew I was sincere. And since then I carried out my promise. Then I told Him I wanted to be filled with His Holy Spirit and I believed very simply that He did it right then. Now I know that when I was saved the Holy Spirit came and lived in me. But He really never had control of all of me. This week I gave Him all of me!

"When I was finished praying I didn't hear any bells ringing, or see any lights flashing—but I felt such calmness and real deep peace! I got up from my knees and opened my Bible. I couldn't believe it. It was the same Bible I had read for years, but suddenly it was very exciting to me. I didn't want to put it down! Verses I'd heard all my life suddenly had significance for me. They applied to me in my life!

"For example, you know John 10:10. It says, 'I am come that you might have life and might have it more abundantly.' That's exactly what He has given me—abundant life. And it's great!

"And Colossians 3:15 says, 'Let the peace of God rule in your heart.' I had never thought of it before, but all I needed was to allow God's peace to take over and control me. It has been ruling in my heart all week, Norm, even when you were late for supper or the children were scrappy. It has been ruling over that awful temper of mine! And God's peace wins out every time!

"Or, John 15:11 that talks about the fullness of joy God would give us. That's how I feel—like I have full and complete joy all day. Or then there's the verse—"

"Hold it a minute, Betty! I understand. I get the idea." I decided I had better stop her before she quoted the whole New Testament to me. "I really don't know what to think or say about it all, but I am happy for you. Yes, I'm really happy for you. I appreciate the changes I've seen in you and—I need to do some thinking—a lot of thinking. Let's call it a night, shall we?"

"Sure, darling. It is a lot to think about, but it's worth the time—believe me!"

The next few days I felt miserable. I felt so empty. Betty continued to be kind and sweet. She seldom raised her voice or nagged. She excitedly shared new Scripture verses with me throughout the day. I started doing a lot of self-examination and calling out to the Lord. I started reading the Bible more. I became convinced that this experience was truly from God, and I sincerely wanted it too. But I wasn't quite ready—not yet.

The next week Betty told me there were going to be some, special services at a church in Steelton, about thirty miles away. Her friends, the Ebersoles, had invited us to go along with them. I guessed I might be in for some preaching along the same lines I had been hearing from Betty for days, and I was reluctant to go.

My fears were well-grounded. When we got to the first service I was amazed to see people clapping their hands, raising their arms and audibly praising the Lord. I couldn't believe it! I was pretty cautious about the whole thing!

But the next evening I was back again. My questions were mounting. Most of the people I met there seemed to have the same radiant expressions on their faces that Betty now had. They had something I didn't have!

By the third and fourth nights I was becoming convinced of what I needed to do, but I wanted to wait until I could talk things out with God in private.

A few nights later Betty was out and the children were all in bed. Everything was quiet and I knew the time had come. Sitting in the living room with my Bible in my lap, I began just as Betty had.

"Lord," I prayed earnestly, "I want you to show me any things in my life that I need to make right. Whatever it is, Lord, I'll do it!" I waited a moment. The names of five people I had wronged came to my mind. It flashed through my mind that they would probably think less of me and trust me less if I confessed my wrongdoing to them. But I had promised God and I wasn't going to turn back now, no matter what anybody said.

I continued, "Lord, just take over in my life and fill me with your Holy Spirit. Thank you, Lord. I believe you have done it already!"

Exactly all that occurred then I can't even remember. I do know that a big change took place. I was always very un-emotional, but for a while my emotions were overflowing as I praised God. The Lord really transformed, or remade my life at that moment. Like Betty, I opened my Bible and couldn't believe what had happened.

I had faithfully read my Bible every day for years, but it had always been a duty I performed, with no great enjoyment. Now it became alive to me. It was talking about me and my situation. It was current and up-to-date.

I couldn't wait to tell Betty! She cried with joy when I shared with her later that evening what had happened to me. We prayed together that night, pouring out our hearts to God in gratitude for our newly-found lives. I felt like we had been united more intimately than ever before, because God through His Spirit had made us truly "one."

It occurred to me that things really weren't any different in my lifetime than they were during Jesus' lifetime on earth. Hebrews 13:8 jumped out at me, "Jesus Christ is the same yesterday, today and forever."

"Betty," I exclaimed, "if Jesus is really the same today, then He can do all the things today, that He did way back in Bible times. That means He can heal today, just as He did then!"

It was like a dazzling ray of hope had just fallen across both of us. Maybe God would be the answer to all our health problems—we had to find out more.

In the days to follow, Betty and I read and reread the Gospels. We wanted to know more about the Jesus who had invaded our lives. The more we read, the more convinced we became. He could heal us and He would heal us if we just asked Him!

We read in John 16:24 (NIV) that we hadn't received because we hadn't asked. That meant we ought to ask God for healing. We'd always been too timid for that before. We were scared it might not be His will. Next, we discovered Philippians 4:6 that says we should ask "with thanksgiving." Now, that was a completely new idea! We never would have thought to do that ourselves. Yet, when I reflected for a bit, I recalled thanking my dad for the car he was going to get me for my birthday, even before I received it. Surely our heavenly Father could be relied on even more to keep His word. Of course we could and should thank Him even before receiving His gifts. Finally we came across Mark 11:21-25 where we are told three times that what we say will come to pass. We had often prayed about our problems, but we never felt confident enough to voice our prayers to others. I guess we figured silence would save ourselves and God some embarrassment when the answers didn't come. The problem was, of course, that we just didn't have faith that God would do it. Now we did! We had faith because we had met Him in a personal way!

So our course of action was clear. We not only would ask Him for healing, but we would thank Him in advance and talk aloud about how He was going to perform just what we had asked.

We decided to believe for Betty first. There was no doubt that her life had changed dramatically. The doctor who had suggested I take her to an institution would not have known her. But we wanted the healing to be complete. So we prayed that the Lord would take away all her need for mood-altering meds! Then we burned them!

It was wonderful! She never needed another one! We were just beginning to taste a little of God's great love for us. It would not have mattered if God never healed anyone, but the fact that He did heal people was like frosting on a cake. Betty's healing was an extra dose of joy on top of the fullness we already had experienced, And what we didn't know was that there was so much more to come! Praise the Lord!

4

More Frosting on the Cake

Life became a joyous experience for us once we made Jesus number one in our lives! For the first time in years we had peace and confidence to face the future. It was as if God himself had planted seeds of contentment in our hearts. Each day He watered them as we prayed and read His Word until they blossomed into the beautiful fruit of security and faith.

There was no way I could forget how shy and withdrawn I had been as a young person. Betty too had always dreaded being asked to say even a few words in front of a handful of other people. But now we had something that made us so happy, we simply could not keep quiet about it. I shared with Betty that my greatest desire was to witness to others about what Jesus had done for us!

I certainly didn't have any sort of public ministry in mind. We still counted on continuing as farmers—striving to deepen our relationships with the Lord in order to become the best parents and mates possible. However, we did have a burning desire to tell those we met about the fulfilling joy we had found.

One day, soon after our life-changing experience with the Lord in 1957, I saw a hitchhiker on the roadside. I had never picked up hitchhikers often—and whenever I did, I always drove in uncomfortable silence and felt relieved when I would deposit the passenger at his destination!

On this particular day I felt a sudden, strong urge to stop for this fellow. It was not an audible voice that told me to stop, I just sensed I had to and I obeyed that inner compulsion.

As we started off down the winding country road, I found myself telling this young traveler how I had just met Jesus Christ in a new and wonderful way. I explained how the Lord had already healed my wife from her emotional illness and how we were confident that He was going to cure our children. Suddenly, a strange thoughtful silence settled over us both. As I glanced at my passenger, I was amazed to see tears streaming down his face. He looked at me with a peculiarly familiar expression. It was that wistful look of hunger—spiritual hunger—a look that said, "Please, Sir, tell me more about Jesus!"

We had a wonderful talk that day! The young man seemed to take in every word I said. Within a half-hour, he had prayed for God's forgiveness and asked Jesus to take control of his life. As I left him off, that sweet sense of peace to which I was becoming accustomed, settled over me. The confidence that was beginning to sprout in my heart assured me that God would be following after that individual and through His Holy Spirit, would be drawing him closer and closer to himself.

It was startling to realize I had done so much talking! I laughed in sheer amazement! In those few minutes with the hitchhiker, I had talked more than I would have in an entire week before receiving the baptism. The transformation God had already brought about in my life was truly incredible!

When as a teen-ager I had first accepted Christ as my Savior from sin, I memorized the verse, "If any man be in Christ he is a new creature . . . old things are passed away, behold all things are become new" (2 Cor. 5:17). I knew my sins were forgiven, but in so many ways my life had not seemed a whole lot different from before. Now I felt as if I had truly been reborn—it was like starting a brand new way of living. It was seeing life from an entirely new perspective.

Both Betty and I marveled at how even the tiniest pleasures of life had become especially meaningful for us. For example, Betty always had been a lover of nature. Even during her emotional ups and downs she would find great delight in a small bouquet of wildflowers or a particularly clear, starry night. Now, she appreciated these wonders even more and would thank the Lord over and over again for the lovely world He had given us.

On one warm September day she was heading out to clean eggs. The wind was refreshing and she was singing and praising God for His goodness. Passing the wash line on her way to the chicken house, she looked up and spotted a brilliant yellow bird perched on the post near her. Betty had always longed for a canary as a child, but her family had been unable to afford one. So, for her, just seeing one tiny yellow bird was a special treat. She was thrilled with the little creature, for she knew they were very scarce in Lancaster County. Imagine her surprise when she took another look and realized there were yellow birds flying toward her from all directions. During the next five minutes about forty yellow birds flew down and surrounded her. Some perched on the wash line, some on the fence. Betty could hardly believe her eyes! She laughed for pure joy! It was as though God had arranged a special show just for her—it was great! Ginger, our dog, wasn't quite so impressed and came bounding over to investigate. The birds were up and away in a flash of sunshiny color! But for Betty, the happiness they had brought, lasted for a long time. She went about the rest of the day's work with a song and a smile. How good God was!

When I returned from the fields that evening, Betty could scarcely control herself long enough to give me the whole story.

"Really?" I asked with raised eyebrows. I was beginning to recognize God as a God of miracles, but "let's face it," I thought, "there just aren't that many yellow birds in this area."

Just then, as if to verify her word and the power of our God, the birds came back. Betty glanced out the window and gave a shout of surprise.

"Norm," she cried, "Just look out there now! See for yourself!"

I jumped up and ran over to the window. There in our yard, was a whole flock of yellow birds fluttering around and singing beautifully. I could not deny it. I had seen them my-self! Betty continued excitedly, "Isn't that just like the Lord? He said if we delight ourselves in Him, He will give us 'the desires of our heart' (Ps. 37:4). He is so good!"

"Lord," I prayed, 'blessed are those who have not seen and yet have believed' (John 20:29). Help me to trust you, even when I haven't seen it with my own eyes!"

There was a lot of opportunity for us to learn to trust the Lord without "seeing!" Since Betty had been healed so miraculously, we were encouraged to believe for the rest of the family's health problems.

Again we simply claimed Heb. 13:8, "Lord, if you are the same today as you were when you walked this earth (and we believe you are!), then you can still heal. We just ask you now to heal our children, in Jesus' name." As we prayed, we laid our hands on our daughter Joann and our son John. In our hearts we felt assured that they would be healed. We thanked God for it in advance!

Immediately Joann was back to normal. Her symptoms and discomfort disappeared. We wanted to verify this and so we took her to the doctor. He was amazed to report no sign of the nephritis which had plagued her. She never had a recurrence! Her kidneys were as good as new!

Next it was Johnny's turn. His fever left and the pain in his joints vanished when we prayed. Betty took him to the heart specialist, Dr. Hoover in Lancaster, for his scheduled appointment. The doctor checked our little fellow over carefully and then turned toward Betty with a puzzled expression on his face.

"I don't understand this, Mrs. Charles," he began slowly. "I can't find a trace of a heart murmur in this boy! There really isn't any reason why he can't go back home and try returning to normal activities. I do suggest however, that he remain on penicillin, until he is grown, or there is the possibility it could recur."

Betty couldn't wait to get home and give me the news! Imagine the profound satisfaction we felt to see Johnny run over and hop on his tricycle. Our little son, who hadn't budged from his hospital bed in months was running and playing again! We did a lot of hugging and crying and shouting that day!

The only thing that concerned me was the message about John's medication. I had been sensing that the Lord wanted me to start tithing—giving Him 10 percent of our income. Yet, the money I was paying for John's penicillin alone, was more than the amount I would need to tithe. Through all our illnesses we had had no hospitalization or insurance. This was in keeping with our church tradition. I was in desperate financial trouble. I just couldn't see how I could possibly tithe.

I headed out behind the barn. There was a spot there which was becoming my own private chapel. I fell on my knees and told the Lord exactly what I was feeling.

"Father," I prayed, "You are so good! You healed Betty and Joann and now Johnny! I praise you and thank you for these miracles, Lord! Now I guess I can't really see how it would be any harder to keep Johnny healed, than it was for you to heal him in the first place. So I'm going to stop John's medication and use that money to pay the 10 percent I owe you. I'm leaving John's continued healing in your hands, Father! And I believe you are going to work everything out fine! How I praise you, Jesus!"

I'm sure some folks may have thought I was being an unwise and neglectful father to do this. To most people it was just plain foolish to ignore the doctor's advice. It was as though I was putting my son's life in jeopardy again. But I was beginning to understand how great His love for me was! And I knew He hadn't done a halfway job. His healing was complete and I felt confident in my heart that it would be permanent.

It was! John never needed penicillin for his heart again! Praise the Lord!

And what's more, as I began to give my tithe to God, He began to bless me financially. The cows gave more milk, the chickens laid more eggs, the farm machinery stayed in good working condition, the crops did well. It overwhelmed me to see how our financial needs were being met, one by one. Many, many times I had to exclaim, "Thank you, Lord! Thank you, Lord—just for who you are—the one who is concerned with every need we face!"

Betty and I eagerly looked forward to the day when God would heal my back as well. We had rejoiced together over all the other healings. Why, God had even healed our pet cow, Jane.

She had been found lying in the pasture one day, unable to get on her feet. When the vet examined her, he said there was nothing that could be done for her. He advised us to sell her to the butcher. When I inquired how they would move her, he explained the usual method. A rope would be tied around her neck and run up through the cattle truck and fastened to a tractor. The tractor would then tow her up onto the truck bed. I cringed to picture our pet cow going through that kind of torture. So, there in the pasture, I knelt down, put my arms around Jane's neck, and asked the Lord to heal her. Before four o'clock the next morning I hurried to the pasture. I couldn't wait to see what had happened! There was Jane, standing with the rest of the cows, munching away contentedly. And what's more, she was the first one that headed back that evening for milking, with not so much as a limp. I roused the whole family so we could praise the Lord together for Jane's healing! The children weren't as surprised as I had anticipated. "Of course Jane's all right, Dad," Johnny remarked matter-of-factly when I awakened him with the news. "You prayed for her, didn't you?!" Our God answers prayer!

Luke Weaver, a dear minister friend, was amazed that God had healed Jane. "After all," he reasoned with God one day, "I pray for a lot of people. Some are healed. Some aren't. I always figured it depended on their faith—but that cow certainly didn't have any faith!" He admitted to me later, with a laugh, that it was as if God plainly answered him, "She didn't have any unbelief either!" That was for sure!

Well, we reasoned that if God was concerned about everyone else in our family and even about our cow, He had to be interested in my problem too. The pain in my back had been getting worse. I knew there was absolutely nothing that could be done on a human level to prevent it. After my fall I had been warned that eventually my back would give out on me. As each day passed, it became more and more evident that that forecast would probably come true.

However, I knew the God who heals! And He had healed so many already! I had no doubt but that He was going to heal me too! Each day Betty and I claimed my healing. Each day I pulled myself agonizingly out of bed, clenched my teeth from the pain and forced myself to endure the work of the day. I could not understand exactly why God did not heal me right away, but I knew He was going to do it, someday. I just had to be patient to wait for His timing.

The weeks passed and months went by. I didn't want to go back to any doctor since I had already tried them all. I would keep on believing God, no matter what.

But the pain got worse. One Sunday evening we had invited all of Betty's family over to the farm for a visit. I loved to make homemade ice cream for a crowd and that night I had cranked the freezer plenty. Then I made the rounds to serve up the ice cream. It required all the self-control I could muster to keep a smile on my face. My back was aching terribly. I just prayed for strength to last through those hours.

The next morning I headed out to the barn as usual to face another week of farm work. But my back was hurting more than ever. I picked up a shovel and dug into my chores.

That's when something snapped! I collapsed in pain! I never could have imagined any person having to endure such agony. It knocked the breath right out of me and I just lay moaning on the barn floor.

Finally it dawned on me that I had to get help, so I struggled to pull myself over to the milk house. It was 5:30 a.m. and calling Betty wouldn't do any good. No one else would be up in the house at that time.

When I reached the milk house, I fell over the milk cooler with my feet dangling. It was the only position that prevented me from fainting. How long I lay there I'm not really sure. But I prayed and waited and finally made a last huge effort to drag myself into the house. The Lord must have helped me because as soon as I reached the sofa in the living room, I collapsed once again in excruciating pain. I called Betty and she came immediately.

For the next several hours any position brought constant pain to me. We called three different doctors and they ordered me to the hospital. I could not understand why God was allowing this, but I just kept telling Him I would trust Him anyway, even if it meant going to the hospital.

So the ambulance came and I was admitted to the hospital. When the doctor checked me, he gave me a shot which he said would certainly kill the pain, as it was the strongest painkiller he could prescribe. It did not do a thing! Then began a series of X-rays. All my life I had always tried to keep up a strong front. I was not a complainer, and whenever I would get sick, I would try to hide the way I was feeling. I liked the he-man image. But this back pain was more than I could control or hide! All anyone had to do was touch my back lightly and I would holler. I felt like a sissy, but I couldn't help it!

Wednesday noon, two days after my collapse, the doctor finally gave me the diagnosis. He explained that the damage to my back was extremely serious—maybe irreparable. I would be put in traction with heavy weights for a few weeks and then in a cast from my neck to my knees for six more weeks. And then the shattering news—there was no guarantee that any of these treatments would help. My back might never support me again!

When the doctor left my room I had another heart-to-heart talk with the Lord. "Father, you are so good to me! I believe you are healing me. Help me to have the patience to wait for your time!"

About four o'clock that afternoon two men walked into my room within thirty seconds of each other. One was Lester Ebersole who had helped us so much in our new spiritual life. The other man was also a good friend, Martin Landis. I was amazed that they had arrived at the same moment for one was from Harrisburg and the other from east of Lancaster and neither one knew the other was coming. It was even more astounding to hear that both of them had felt led by the Lord to come and pray for my healing that afternoon.

I expressed my gratitude for their concern and I was happy to let them pray for me. But I reminded them that I had been claiming healing all along for myself and as of yet my back seemed no better.

Nevertheless, they read a couple of Scripture verses and then laid their hands on me to pray. Betty, expecting a loud, fervent prayer, suggested they close the door, lest the noise disturb those in the hallway. Lester assured her it wasn't necessary. They very simply asked the Lord to heal me and then thanked Him. It was no earth-shattering kind of prayer. They chatted a bit more with us and left.

I didn't feel different. I continued to shift my weight around in bed, trying desperately to find some means of relieving the discomfort.

But early that evening I became aware that the pain had lessened. I settled into a more comfortable position, thanking God for easing my suffering. As the minutes and hours ticked by, the discomfort diminished. I could feel my body relaxing. I could feel the pressure in my spine disappearing. My excitement was mounting and I just kept praising the Lord over and over for what was happening!

By midnight I had no pain at all!! I wanted to jump right up and shout to everybody what God had done for me! Instead,

I just praised and worshiped the Lord in the quietness of my room. He had stood true to His Word again—how good He was to me! I was so delightfully happy I just wanted to stay awake and praise the Lord! But finally I dropped off to sleep—the first restful night I had spent in years!

In the morning I knew beyond the shadow of any doubt that my back was completely well! I could not wait to tell the doctor! When he walked in, I immediately blurted out, "Doc, the Lord healed me last night!"

He looked at me like I was crazy. He probably figured the pain had been too much for me and I was going into shock. But he also knew I had not been able to talk without moaning before. Now I was bright and alert and moving my body without wincing.

He did not say another word, just turned and walked out. About two minutes later he was back again with another doctor. I repeated my good news to him. He gave me the same puzzled look, but at least he began examining me, along with the first doctor.

Just touching my back the day before had caused me to cry out from intense pain, but now they could poke me anywhere and it simply did not hurt at all. They checked me out thoroughly and I could tell they were getting more perplexed by the minute.

They left again and returned with a stretcher. I was to be taken down to the dispensary. It would have been simple for me to climb onto the stretcher myself, but they insisted on moving me very carefully to the other bed. Inwardly I was chuckling! When we arrived at the dispensary all my X-rays were displayed and a group of doctors were discussing them. There was no doubt from looking at those pictures that my back had been in terrible shape. No wonder it was so hard for them to figure out how I could possibly be feeling so well.

One doctor came over to examine me again. Then he asked, "Do you think you could sit up?"

"Sure I can!" I volunteered cheerfully. Up I sat without any problem.

"Could you stand, do you think?" he continued cautiously.

"Sure!" And down I hopped. He grabbed onto me as I climbed down, but I certainly didn't need any assistance.

"Do you think you could walk?" It was as though he wished I would say "no" to one of his questions—at least that would have been easier to explain.

But I responded with another enthusiastic, "Of course I can walk!" And I walked right out into the hall. There were two doctors at my heels with a wheelchair. Evidently they figured I would collapse at any moment. But I did not! God does not do things halfway. I knew that! And I knew I was healed! Praise the Lord!

Well, they weren't giving me any more instructions. They were speechless! So, I proceeded to the elevator to go back up to my room. The two doctors remained right behind me. That elevator ride seemed to take forever. No one said a word! I just kept grinning and silently praising the Lord. The doctors stared awkwardly at the floor. They were obviously deep in thought.

When the elevator doors slid open, I headed back to my room and the doctors went in the opposite direction with the wheelchair. They were convinced I wasn't going to be needing it!

A few moments later one of the doctors returned. I was anxious to hear his report. I wanted to go home and I did not see any reason why they would want to keep me any longer. Unfortunately his news was not so positive. He warned me gravely that I was to get back into bed and stay flat on my back for the next twenty-four hours. They were expecting me to suffer a relapse at any moment. There was no convincing him that I was permanently well.

I did as I was told, very reluctantly! "Why should I be flat on my back when I could be walking around?" I mused, a little disgustedly.

One hour passed and my own family doctor strode through the door of my room.

"Hey, doc, did you know the Lord healed me?" I beamed.

"Yeah, I've been hearing about it all over this place!" he replied with an amused twinkle in his eye. "Listen, I don't pretend to understand what happened, but we've decided to let you get up and do whatever you feel well enough to do. Today's Thursday. If there is no change for the worse by Saturday, you can go home."

That was the kind of news I wanted to hear. "Thank you, Jesus." I whispered contentedly.

As soon as the doctor left, I grabbed my robe and slippers and hurried into the hall. I noticed Dr. Rigano and some nurses standing around the reception desk. The nurses were laughing. It was apparent from the direction of their glances that they had been discussing me. As I drew closer I heard the doctor's words, "Well, you must admit that a higher power took over in this situation."

"I'll say a higher power took over," I laughed to myself. "No one on earth could have done what the Lord just did for me!"

That was Thursday. I was to be released on Saturday. During those final two days in the hospital I made my own rounds. I shared what Jesus had done with anyone who would listen! Some people got angry. Some cried. They all listened. And they heard, many for the first time, that God cares about us and loves us and wants to help us in our need.

On Saturday morning, two men strolled down the hall. I recognized them immediately as the ambulance attendants who had brought me to the hospital. They looked at me with strange expressions.

"Aren't you the one we brought in here on Monday?" one of them asked hesitantly.

"I sure am!" I replied with a laugh, "but let me tell you what Jesus did!" I repeated the story once more and before I finished, they had tears in their eyes. They could hardly believe it, and yet they had to admit it must be true. They had seen the difference with their own eyes. They were facing up to the fact that there is a God who cares!

I suddenly realized why the Lord had allowed me to come to the hospital. There were dozens of people who had needed to hear that Jesus loved them and wanted to live in them. I

71

was humbled to realize that God had chosen to use my illness to get that message to them. What a great God!

True to their promise, the doctors released me on Saturday. It was super to walk back into our house, straight and tall!

And it was great to sit in church the next day! Why, I hardly even noticed the hard benches! My excitement kept spilling out and before church was over, everyone had heard what God had done for me. I simply could not keep the goodness of the Lord to myself! Quiet old me, who never would have dreamed of speaking in front of a group, was bubbling over with joy!

Betty was just as ecstatic as I was! She suddenly found herself with a young husband again. And of course, since she herself was so joyful now, we made a pretty enthusiastic couple.

We grabbed every opportunity to share what God had done for us and we felt sure that everyone would be thrilled to listen. We soon discovered however, that not all wanted to hear. I guess some felt we were preaching at them. We certainly didn't want to make anyone feel condemned. More than anybody, we knew just how undeserving we were of God's love. That was what was so absolutely wonderful to us—God had saved us, filled us with His Spirit, healed us and transformed our lives—all this in spite of the fact that we did not deserve it one bit! But when we took just one tiny step toward Him, He took a giant leap toward us! That was news worth sharing!

One evening in our home we had been sharing with several guests what the Lord meant to us! Betty was always the more talkative of the two of us, and as she rambled on,

I observed the reactions of a few of the visitors. Some were really soaking in her words, but there were at least a couple that seemed rather "turned off." I thought they looked uncomfortable and sort of disgusted.

When the guests left, I decided to discuss the matter with Betty.

"Sunshine," I began, patting her hand, "you and I both know what the Lord has done for us and what He still is doing. And the Lord knows we can't thank Him enough for everything. But I'm beginning to wonder if we haven't been coming on a bit too strong for some folks. We had better back off from sharing so much, or we may do more harm than good."

"Okay, Norm. I think you're probably right. But it makes me feel miserable to think about keeping quiet, when the Lord could help others too!" Betty left the room with her Bible under her arm.

A few minutes later she rushed into the kitchen and grabbed my arm. "Look at this!" she urged. She was holding her Bible open, pointing to a verse.

"What's up, Betty?"

"I really thought you must be right to suggest we should not talk so much about the Lord, but I felt so sad. I decided I would read a little from the Bible to cheer me up. And look at the verse I opened to!"

I read aloud, "We cannot help speaking about what we have seen and heard" (Acts 4:20 NIV).

I threw back my head and laughed. "All right, I give up! The Lord knows best and if He says it's okay for us to keep on talking—well, that's great with me!" Needless to say, we've been sharing ever since!

Sometimes it has gotten us into a little trouble. There were occasional times of opposition. But mostly our sharing has been received with a look of hunger—that deep desire to know and experience more of God's reality. And what satisfaction we felt, seeing people turn to Him to find the fullness of joy we had found in Him too! This was life well worth the living!!

5

Upshot of a One-Ton Fleece

One thing we discovered when we put God first was that we didn't need to go hunting opportunities for sharing about Jesus. The opportunities just kept coming, in various and surprising ways.

For example, through all our problem years Betty and I had been very quiet in church. We certainly were not looked up to as leaders. We were the "poor souls" who had so much sickness and debt. People pitied us, chided us, and advised us, but no one ever sought our counsel on anything. And why should they have? We certainly had no answers!

Now Jesus had become the answer to our problems. We could not keep quiet about what He had done. And amazingly, folks began coming to us and asking questions. At first they were just innocent, curiosity-type questions. Soon the curiosity of the people changed to longing and their questioning into prayer requests. People began pouring out the yearnings of their hearts to us. The hypocrisy they had hidden behind for years, the secret sins they were harboring and their deep craving to know a living Jesus were admitted openly to us. We simply helped them find Him—the Jesus who could transform lives through the power of His Holy Spirit!

Our old-fashioned parlor became a meeting place—a place where people met God. Friends started dropping in to share about spiritual matters and request prayer. Sometimes they invited others and before long we were having prayer and praise meetings in our home several times each week. Individuals were accepting Christ and praying to receive the baptism of the Holy Spirit, or physical healing. We became more and more aware that God knew no limitation as to the number and seriousness of needs He could handle. In Gen. 18:14 we read, "Is anything too hard for the Lord?" He could perform the impossible! We began to see more and more changed lives. It was exciting!

When our church asked us to teach Sunday school we could scarcely believe our ears! What was even more surprising was the classes we were asked to take. They wanted Betty to teach senior high girls and I was to teach the senior high boys. The boys were notorious for being hard on their teachers!

We prayed about it and felt the Lord showed us we were to take the classes. "After all," we reasoned, "if these young people would really give their lives to Jesus in their teen years, they could be spared so much of the struggle and grief we had to suffer." We decided to share with these teenagers just what we were learning from the Bible. Studying and learning together, we hoped they would catch some of our excitement.

Love began to spring up between these kids and us! They did not seem to mind how unsophisticated and uneducated we were. Genuineness mattered most to them. They had undoubtedly heard about us before we began teaching, and were probably a bit curious to observe these "fanatics." But as we opened up the Bible and shared with sincerity and fervor that God's Word really is true, they responded with the same hunger we had observed so often. Many of them committed their lives to the Lord and began a new way of life.

We felt we could not have been more happy, unless we had been in heaven face to face with Jesus. In fact, we were beginning to understand that Jesus wants to be so real and so near to us here on earth, that our daily life can become a foretaste of heaven. The Bible says, "the upright shall dwell in His presence" (Ps. 140:13). I am sure this verse does not refer only to heaven. Here and now, when we obey Him, we can be living in His presence! That's tremendous!

It was not long, however, till we discovered that the more determined we were to follow Jesus, the more attacks Satan made to try to trip us up! For example, we had made up our minds that our whole family was going to be in church each Sunday. For years either Betty or I had had to stay home with a sick child almost every week.

We realized now that it was important for our children to be in church, so we told the Lord we were determining to start church attendance as a "whole" family.

Wouldn't you know? The first week after we made that decision the twins came down with fever late that Saturday night. Betty sighed resignedly.

"Guess I'll have to stay home with Mervin and Marvin," she said with a tired shrug.

"No, you won't be staying home with them," I announced. She looked at me with a questioning stare. "I'm not staying home with them either, so don't look at me like that," I responded. "We made a promise to the Lord and we're going to keep it. 'No matter how many promises God has made, they are yes in Christ!' (2 Cor. 1:20 NIV) "He doesn't back out on His promises to us. We're going to start following through on our word to Him too! Eccles. 5:4 tells us, 'When you make a vow to God, do not delay in fulfilling it' (NIV). We'll pray for the boys and believe the Lord to heal them. But come morning, fever or not, we're all going to church!"

Come morning the fever had lessened some. We scurried around in a manner similar to most households on Sunday morning. By the time we arrived at church the twins' fevers were completely gone and they were as peppy and cheerful as ever. "Thank you, Lord!" Betty and I echoed together. "You've done it again!"

The hardest opposition we faced came from right within our own church. There were some people who just didn't like to hear us talking about and praising the Lord so much. At one point in our lives we had questioned such things too!

Though we could understand their feelings, we just couldn't keep silent. We already knew what the Lord had to say about that! We had to speak the things we had heard and seen ourselves. A little criticism wasn't going to hurt us anyway. Jesus had suffered from the misunderstanding and criticism of others too. We committed it to the Lord and determined not to hold bitterness in our hearts.

Nevertheless, it was more difficult when approximately one year after receiving the baptism of the Holy Spirit, the criticism came in the form of an ultimatum. It was kindly, but firmly "suggested" to us that we hold no more "home" prayer meetings and attend no other services outside our own church. Failure to comply with these suggestions would result in loss of our church membership.

How we thanked the Lord for the Mennonite church! It had been in this denomination that Betty and I had learned good honest, moral values. It was there that we had accepted Christ as Savior when just young teens. It was there that we had been taught the Bible stories which just now were beginning to take on great significance in our lives. It was where many of our friends and relatives worshiped. To leave would be terribly difficult—like amputating parts of our own bodies. But to stay, we would have had to refuse to help the people who were coming into our home each week. We just could not find any verse in Scripture that taught it was wrong to pray with other believers in your own home. In fact, in Acts, we found several examples which would indicate the exact opposite.

Again we prayed. Gradually we came to the decision that to leave the church quietly, would be the best course of action. We certainly did not want to be a source of dissension in the church! Wonderfully, the Lord gave us a deep inner peace about the matter. He gave us the freedom to leave without hostility or resentment and miraculously our relationship with many of the church members improved in the following months, in spite of the fact that we were no longer worshiping at the same place. We could not have known then, but years later we were to be invited back into many Mennonite churches, including our own home congregation, to share what the Lord had done for us! He is so good!

We had heard it said that the Lord never closes one door without opening another. In the months following our withdrawal from the Mennonite church, I could not escape the growing conviction that the Lord was leading us to the mission field.

I remember when the thought first crossed my mind. I dismissed it in a jiffy. "We're too old; we have no training and besides Betty would never consider leaving her friends and relatives!" The subject was closed.

At least to me it was, but not to God. While working out in the fields I was impressed again and again that we were to be missionaries. Plowing took longer than usual as I argued with the Lord about the whole matter.

"In the first place, Lord, we're both thirty-four years old. That's too old to begin a whole new way of life. We have never been to Bible school, and no school would accept us anyway, since we never even finished high school. We have too many children and a horrible health record. No mission board in its right mind would consider sending our family. I have too many debts to pay yet and I couldn't consider going with a long list of outstanding bills. We've never mastered the English language correctly, let alone a foreign tongue. And finally, Lord," (and this to me was the clincher) "Betty would never agree to it. Of that I'm positive."

I had assured myself that the matter was settled. But that gnawing, uncomfortable feeling continued. I simply could not shake it off.

Some weeks went by. We were busy helping others. I kept reasoning to myself that we were missionaries right in our own part of Pennsylvania. We did not have to go overseas—there were plenty of needs all around us.

That was true enough, but it was still a "cop-out." Day after day, the words of a song kept running through my mind. It was a song the Lord had given me right after I had been filled with the Holy Spirit. I had been out in the barn, milking cows, when suddenly this song just overcame me (and believe me, I am no musician). Since that day, it had never ceased resounding in my mind. The lyrics were simple, but the message compelling:

> The fields are ripe, all ready to harvest.
> So why are the reapers so few?
> If you're not a reaper, you must be to harvest,
> So may God help you today.
> Come to Jesus today!
> Give your all to Him!
> He'll take and cleanse you,
> Fill and use you
> In His harvest plan.

Was God really calling me to be a reaper for Him in some faraway country? It seemed He was and I knew I could not refuse Him much longer.

One sunshiny afternoon in the early summer of 1959, I discussed the whole thing once again with the Lord, while bumping along on the tractor. "Okay," I conceded, "I think you're telling me that we're to be missionaries—and, Lord, I really do want to obey you no matter what! So, if that's what you want, I'll do it. But you also know you'll have to convince Betty. I'm positive I could never persuade her—in fact, it will probably be some job for you too—no offense, Lord! I just don't think she will go for the idea at all. But I'm going to trust you, Father, and thanks for working this all out!"

That evening, after the children were peacefully asleep, I told Betty I wanted to discuss something. We poured ourselves some freshly brewed coffee and sat down comfortably at the kitchen table. It was the favorite conference spot for our family.

Betty looked at me expectantly. "Okay, you've got me curious. What's on your mind?"

She was almost glowing with excitement and I really figured she was in for a big letdown. But I had promised the Lord and I intended to follow through. I took a long sip from my mug and reached over to take her hand. Silently I prayed, "Lord, help me to say this right!"

I began, "Sunshine, the Lord has been talking to me about something lately. I feel He may be wanting us to make a change."

"What sort of change?" Her question held no fear that I could detect. In fact, she seemed, well—almost eager. I plunged on.

"Well, remember the story of Abraham and how God called him to leave his relatives and hometown to go to a country that God would show Him? (Gen. 12:1). The Lord seems to be talking to me like that—saying we should be willing to leave our family and friends and go to the mission field to serve Him. Now, I can understand, Betty, how hard that would be for—"

"Norm, wait a minute." Betty interrupted me with a giggle. "It wouldn't be hard for me if I was convinced that God was really calling us to do that. And as far as I'm concerned—I'm already convinced!"

I guess I just sat there looking dumbfounded for a minute. Then in disbelief I asked, "You mean you think we're supposed to be missionaries too?"

"Yes, I do. I've been feeling the Lord talking to me about it for months, but I simply didn't have the courage to bring the subject up to you. I was positive you'd never be willing to leave the farm. It always has been your whole life. So I just kept trying to put the entire idea out of my mind. But I couldn't. Finally today I decided to have a long talk with the Lord about it."

"Oh, one of those, huh?" I nodded, grinning. "I had one of those long talks with the Lord today too! But what did you talk about?"

"This whole deal about being missionaries. I finally told Him I was absolutely willing to go, but I wanted to be sure it was His will, and not just some wild notion of my own. I believed the Lord would direct through you, my husband, if He truly wanted us to go. So, I asked the Lord to give me a sign tonight, if going to the mission field was really His will for us. I asked Him to make you bring up the subject and also mention the story of Abraham as an example. That would give me the assurance I needed. Well, you know what just happened!"

It was one of those priceless moments, when we both had to sit in awe-filled silence. We hugged each other tightly and thanked the Lord for His clear guidance in our lives. How we marveled at the supernatural working of our God! He was fitting everything together just perfectly—like a beautiful, complex jigsaw puzzle. He had everything planned out ahead of time. He just had to wait for us to put in the last piece—our willingness to obey His leading! I was deeply moved!

Betty and I talked till very late that night. We felt we were on the verge of opening a very new and very adventurous chapter of our lives. But we would have to cling closely to the Lord all the way. This would be no small undertaking for a couple of simple country folks like us. It would have to be God's hand leading and providing all the way!

In the next week I thought of little else but the possibility of going to the mission field. I had to admit that deep inside there still lurked a bit of doubt. Could it really be that God wanted this? Rationally, it seemed crazy.

Then it was like the Lord gave me a suggestion: "Try me and see if I can't show you unmistakably that you are to be missionaries."

"Okay, Lord," I answered, almost without stopping to think. "I'll put out a fleece like Gideon did in the Bible (Judg. 6:36-39). What should it be, Lord?" The answer came clearly to my mind. "Lord, you know I've still got lots of bills to pay and if we're going to be leaving here I've got to get them paid before we go—so if you make the cows give one thousand pounds more milk this month than last month, then I'll believe beyond a shadow of a doubt, that we're to be missionaries." That was it! That was my fleece!

Almost right away I was amazed at what I had said. I began to consider the enormity of that request. Our herd had just come through its peak month of milk production. There was no way by human standards (or cow standards either) that they could increase their milk production now. They were already starting their downward trend. Still, God could do anything and He knew how important it was for me to be absolutely sure about this step. I was not going to pack up my wife and children and land up in some savage country unless I was positive God wanted us there. So, I let the fleece stand as I had said it, incredible as it seemed, and waited to see what the end of the next month would reveal.

By the end of two weeks I knew milk production was higher than usual. I was beginning to get excited! I half expected things to slow down though. But they did not! The cows just kept giving more and more milk—more than they ever had before!

When it came the end of the month, our records showed unmistakably—the cows had given one thousand pounds more milk than they had given in the previous peak month. What's more, the profit from this miracle enabled me to pay off several bills. We were starting to see light at the end of our tunnel of debt.

You would think I would have gone out and announced to everyone that we were leaving for foreign missionary service. But I did not do so. I had another talk with the Lord. It went something like this: "Lord, I thank you and praise you for showing me your will so clearly. And well—I hope you won't think I'm a terribly slow and troublesome son, but just to make me doubly sure, would you do the same thing again next month for us?"

Had I been the Lord, I think I probably would have shaken my head, shrugged my shoulders and given up on Norm Charles. But God's not like that! He understands us better than anyone in the whole universe. He knew I needed the reassurance and He cared enough for me to do it again!

That's right! The next month the cows gave one thousand pounds extra milk again! This time I would not question Him. I just praised and glorified the Lord for His miraculous leading! How kind and loving a Father He is!

Betty and I had a lot of praying, planning and preparing to do. First, we needed to know where God wanted us to go. We had several friends who were missionaries in Korea and that really appealed to us. Yet, we both felt impressed to go to the land of Brazil. We knew only one Brazilian missionary couple, Lester and Lois Ebersole, who had first introduced us to the baptism of the Holy Spirit. Later we would find out that Lester and Lois had been praying fervently for more missionaries in that land.

Brazil wouldn't have been our natural choice. Somehow we envisioned savage warriors, jungles and panthers whenever Brazil was mentioned. (How uneducated we were!) However, that quiet inner voice which we were coming to recognize as the direction of the Holy Spirit, was without doubt convincing us that Brazil was to be our new home. I guess the Lord was answering the prayers of Lester and Lois by directing us there. Betty and I began to plan for our trip to Brazil.

There was much to do and since we had no previous experience with such matters, we had no idea how much work would be involved in an international move. First, I knew I would have to get our finances straightened out. The extra milk the Lord had miraculously supplied certainly helped us to pay our debts. In fact, the Lord had been prospering us in so many ways that it wasn't long till we were in the "black" again! After thirteen long years of fighting debt—what a relief!

We began to calculate how much money we would need to move to South America. We started working and saving toward that goal. That's when I made a big mistake!

I came home from a farm sale one day, feeling very confused. Word had been spreading about our proposed plans and everywhere I went people were talking about it. At the sale a Christian man came up to me.

"Hey, Norm, I hear talk of you being a missionary but I don't believe it. It's not true, is it?"

"Sure is," I replied enthusiastically. "The Lord's leading us to Brazil. We just want to obey Him and do whatever He tells us."

"What mission board are you going with?"

I hesitated a minute. "Well, actually we're not going under any board. We're just trusting the Lord to guide us and take care of us," I concluded confidently.

"I can't figure how you could ever do a thing like that! How in the world do you plan to support your family? Don't you know the Bible says that a man who doesn't provide for his family is worse than an infidel? If you ask me, you ought to do some more praying. Seems the Lord wouldn't ask you to do something which would hurt your family so much!" He waited for me to answer, but I did not have anything to say. His words had really caught me off guard. One thing was for sure—I really loved my family—and I had always worked hard to be a good provider for them.

"What if we got down there and no support money came? What if the children were miserable? What if they didn't get a good education? What if they got sick and—" My thoughts raced on in one direction—doubt!

By the time I parked the car in our garage, I had come to a conclusion. It would not be easy to tell Betty, but the sooner I got it over with the better.

"Betty, I need to talk to you," I announced as I stepped through the kitchen door, letting the screen bang behind me. Startled, she looked up from setting the table.

"Sorry, I didn't mean to surprise you like that. I've been doing some thinking and I want to know your opinion too." I proceeded to tell her what the man had said to me at the sale. "So maybe it was good he said those things because it got me to consider our plans further. Maybe we've been wrong, or just a little overanxious to minister for the Lord—now that He's been prospering us so much. Our debts are paid, the farm is doing great, we're even saving some money. So, I've been thinking—maybe God wants us to stay home and just give extra money to missions. After all, we've heard enough missionaries say they couldn't be on the field without the gifts of people back here. Maybe that's our way of being missionaries."

Betty was quiet; she focused her eyes on the floor. "Well, if that's what you've been feeling, maybe we ought to give it more consideration. I thought we knew positively that going to Brazil was God's will for us, but now that you say this—well, I'd just never thought of that possibility either. It sounds reasonable enough, I guess, but I'm a little doubtful. Anyway, waiting a little wouldn't hurt and in the meantime we can make certain what God really wants us to do."

We did not have to wait long for that! That very week I noticed peculiar symptoms in some of my cows. Experience had taught me that you don't wait too long to call in the vet. So I had him come right over. He examined the sick cows and his news was not encouraging. They had picked up a disease which had already hit several herds in our area. The vet's prognosis was grim. The disease could spread through the rest of the herd. The affected cows could very well die. Even if they survived, their milk production would be greatly reduced until after their next calves. There went my budding prosperity!

When the vet left, I rushed out behind the barn and fell on my knees. I didn't even know what to say to the Lord. I felt stunned by the vet's words. But suddenly, I heard the Lord saying sternly but gently to me, "You asked me for two signs about going to Brazil and I gave them to you. You yourself felt convinced of the call to Brazil and were willing to obey. Norm, just as I blessed you for your obedience, so easily I can remove that blessing if you disobey."

It was a humbling moment. "Lord," I cried out, "please forgive me! I'll never doubt my call again! We're going to follow you wherever you lead! Right now that means following you to Brazil. We won't turn back again, Lord. I promise!"

Believe it or not, the cows recovered almost immediately and returned to full milk production. I learned some very valuable lessons through that whole experience. First, I learned that we shouldn't doubt God's Word. When He says something He means it. The Bible says, "God is not a man that He should lie, nor a son of man that He should change His mind" (Num. 23:19 NIV).

And I was impressed even more deeply that everything we have is a gift from God. Here I thought I would be "helping God out" by my gifts to missions. In reality every penny I had was from Him! I needed His help, not the other way around. I had doubted His ability to support our family in Brazil. Now I realized that even here in the United States, it was God who supported us! How true the verse is which says, "Every good and perfect gift is from above and cometh down from the Father of lights" (James 1:17). Every blessing we enjoy is a result of His love and care for His children. Without Him, we would have a very sorrowful existence. But with Him we have life abundant! What a wonderful Father!

We began immediately to make preparations for our trip. We wanted to take as little baggage as possible. Since we didn't know if we would ever be returning to the United States to live, we also decided to sell as many of our belongings as possible. It would be unnecessary then, to store a lot of items.

The most practical idea seemed to be to hold a public auction to dispose of our possessions. I began praying about this and asked the Lord when the best time for the auction would be. He impressed on me, "New Years Day!" Now, I was learning that God's ways are not always our ways, but even so, this seemed very risky. New Year's Day in Pennsylvania is infamous for snow, ice and bitter cold.

Still, God had been teaching me not to question Him, but simply to trust. So I did not argue. The announcement was made public that the sale would be on January 1, 1960.

Again news traveled fast, as it always does in rural communities. Again people said we were crazy! This time, though, I didn't listen. I believed God knew what He was doing! So I simply assured people that God was going to bless us with a beautiful day for the sale! As the day approached, many people expressed their doubts. The December weather did not help their faith either. Nevertheless, January 1 dawned bright and sunny! God had done it again! Praise His name!

Over one thousand people came to the sale that day! I know a lot of them did not come to buy. They came because they had heard of the "fanatics" who were moving to South America. They wanted to get a glimpse of these "oddballs" But we were so happy and rejoicing in the Lord that it wasn't even difficult to part with our treasured possessions. I had wondered how Betty would react when it came down to selling wedding presents and other sentimental items. But she walked around with such a look of radiance and peace! People must have thought she looked more like a woman about to gain the whole world, rather than one who (in their estimation) was about to lose it!

Folks strolled around outside without coats that day! Imagine, January 1 and men were outside in short sleeves. Only God could have arranged things so perfectly!

Following the sale we went to live with Betty's sister, Ruth, and her family. Ruth, her husband Roy, and all the children were such an encouragement to us. Inwardly, they were dreading the time when we would have to say goodbye, yet they managed to display such cheerful dispositions, that we tended to forget how soon we would leave the United States—maybe never to return!

We had been saving for our tickets to Brazil and when the funds were finally a little more substantial, I drove down to the travel agency to book our passage. When I informed the agent that we were going to Brazil to live and work as missionaries, he looked interested. "And when do you wish to travel to Brazil, Mr. Charles?" he asked politely.

"Well, we'd like to leave sometime near the beginning of March." I didn't tell him, but the Lord had impressed this on me too! I was completely confident that this was God's scheduled time for us to leave.

He looked startled for a moment and then continued, "But do you have your visa and passport, Sir?" I hated to display my ignorance, but I did not even know what a visa or passport was, let alone that I needed to have them. Remember, we were just simple folks who had never traveled far from home before. I shifted in my chair.

When the agent realized that these requirements were unknown to me, he shook his head in disbelief. "I'm sorry, Mr. Charles, but it takes a long time to get passports and visas. I'm afraid you would never have them in time, even if you applied for them now!" He started to close his schedule books.

I did some quick thinking and breathed a prayer for help. "Would you be able to tell me what I have to do in order to get passports and visas?" When he nodded, I continued, "Then could we go ahead and book a voyage anyway. You see, I believe we're supposed to go in March and so I'm sure God will supply the necessary documents in time."

Again he looked up at me in disbelief! I began sharing with him what God had done in our lives. I could tell his interest was growing. When I paused, he started in kindly to explain the whole document process to me. Then he told me there would be an American freighter ship leaving for Brazil on March 13. That suited me just perfectly and because it was a freighter, it would cost less. I told him I wanted to book passage for seven!

"Seven!" he gasped. "You mean there are more than just you and your wife?"

"Sure, didn't I tell you? My whole family is going. We have five children—a 13-year-old girl, Joann, 11-year-old Jim, eight-year-old Johnny and five-year-old twin boys named Marvin and Mervin!" I beamed with pride!

"Well, I'm sorry, but this shipping line has a policy that it will not accept many children as passengers. This is due to the fact that there is no doctor on board. They can't take responsibility for children's health and safety on board ship for such a long time. You are aware, aren't you, Mr. Charles, that this voyage will be approximately twenty-three days in duration?"

This ticket purchasing hadn't turned out to be as easy as I had expected, but I plunged on, "Yes, I know it will be a long trip—but I'm sure it will be exciting for my children. And about the children—well, we'll take our own Doctor along!"

For a moment, I thought he was actually going to ask me if that meant an eighth ticket was necessary. Then his quizzical expression changed to a slow smile of understanding spreading across his face. He chuckled. "Sir, I'll see what I can do for you, although I can't promise anything. The final decision is with the shipping company. But personally," he hesitated, groping for the right words, "I hope you, your family and your doctor are all accepted for this voyage!"

I grinned and left the office. "Thank you, Jesus," I sang out. "I know we're as good as on our way now!"

Sure enough, the visas and passports came through and finally acceptance from the shipping company arrived. We were to send the money for the tickets in advance. The letter named the deadline for getting the fare to them.

That deadline approached swiftly and we were still short some money—five hundred dollars to be exact. Betty and I discussed the situation. There was no doubt in our minds about going—and we were certain this was the ship on which we were to travel. But we just didn't have the money for the tickets yet.

Again, I felt the Lord speaking to me. He was simply reminding me to "Keep on trusting." I knew what He wanted me to do.

On the morning the payment was to be postmarked, Betty and I sat down at the kitchen table with our checkbook between us. I wrote out the check to Moore-McCormick Shipping Lines for the total amount of the fare, dated that day. Betty was scared, but she put it in a properly-addressed envelope and sealed it. "Lord," I said quietly, "You have a little problem here! It's not my problem! It's yours because you told me we're to sail on that ship. I've worked hard and tried to save. So, we're just going to leave it in your hands now. Thank you, Lord, for working it out! You always do!"

I walked out to the mailbox, at peace in my heart that God was going to supply—somehow! When the postman arrived later he picked up our letter to the shipping company and delivered our incoming mail for the day. When we opened one of the letters, we jumped with joy! In it was a check for five hundred dollars! Jesus had answered again! One thing we were learning—He was never late with His answers. He might not be early either, but at least He was never late! And life sure was exciting with Him in control!

We were going to Brazil! The last few weeks raced by. There was the excitement of final packing, visits from friends and relatives, daydreaming of new adventures awaiting us. But there was also the heartache of knowing we would be saying goodbye to so many loved ones. I can honestly say that after the Lord convinced me He wanted us in Brazil, I never had another fear or reservation about going. But I knew it wasn't so easy for everyone else in the family. Betty loved her family dearly and it would be hard for her to be separated from them, in spite of the fact that she was glad to do God's will. Joann was thirteen and old enough to feel as if she too was being called as a missionary to Brazil. So for her, the trip held much adventure and challenge. For Jim it would be more difficult and I could understand why. He, of all our children, loved the farm the most. He was the one who had dreamed of one day taking over the farm responsibility. Now we had left that special place. We would be leaving his pet dog, Ginger, too—and that would make him sad. I prayed earnestly for Jim during those days. Johnny and the twins were young enough that they would adjust quickly to a new home and new friends. They would be sad to go, but once the goodbyes were said, I was sure they would be fine.

The day before our departure, we faced one final attempt by the enemy to get us to abandon the whole idea. Little Johnny became terribly sick. He had a very high fever and just lay tired and listless in bed. Betty's sister Ruth tried her best to dissuade us from going. "You just can't take a sick boy like John on such a trip!" she warned. And we were just as concerned as she was. But we also had that sweet peace in our hearts that God had called us—and had called us for that particular voyage. So we prayed and believed.

The next day John was fine!

A whole group of our friends and family had chartered a bus to New York, so they could see us off. It was sort of a sorrowful bus ride, saying all our final farewells. Had we known then that we would be home for furloughs it would not have been nearly so difficult. But in our minds, we had no assurance that we would ever return to the United States.

When we arrived at the New York docks, our pastor friend, Luke Weaver, conducted a brief farewell service for us right there on the wharf. It must have caught the attention of the shipping crew, because after the service, they offered to give everyone a special tour of the boat. It was a delightful treat for our relatives and friends!

The bus finally pulled away and as we watched their dear, familiar faces fade from view, we sensed God's hand of love holding us. We gathered the children together and there on the deck of the ship we prayed that this voyage would be an especially happy time for our family. We were following the Lord and He would give us all joy in our new home. We were sure of it!

As the ship pulled out from New York harbor, we gazed back at the shoreline of our homeland and wondered if we would ever see it again. Then, with peaceful hearts and God's courage springing up in our spirits, we all began singing as a family,

> We have decided to follow Jesus,
> We have decided to follow Jesus,
> We have decided to follow Jesus,
> No turning back, no turning back.

No turning back now! We were headed for Brazil, by command of our Captain—JESUS!

6

We No Speaka Portuguese!

The water sparkled like millions of tiny diamonds under the brightness of the sun. It was refreshingly cool on deck and I gazed in awe at the expanse of water on all sides of us. It was breathtaking! Imagine, just the first day of our voyage and already all we could see was ocean all around us. I was full of excitement and anticipation. In three weeks we would be in Brazil! I could hardly wait! Yet, in the meantime, we would have the thrill of an ocean voyage. We had brought games along and since there were very few passengers, we were already being given royal treatment. The children were special favorites of the crew and other guests. I was thankful for all the added attention they were getting. Surely it would help them over their initial sadness about leaving home.

I could not understand why people had warned us so much about seasickness before we left. When I first saw our ship sitting at the New York wharf I thought to myself, "You can't tell me that waves can rock a big thing like that!" I never would have imagined that a ship could be so huge. And now, standing on deck and feeling the gentle rolling, I was convinced that seasickness must be some psychological ailment. We certainly weren't going to have any trouble with it!

My confidence, however, was short-lived! On the second day, a storm blew up. I discovered I never had imagined how big waves could be! At first it was a lot of fun! The children and I laughed and carried on as the ship rose and fell. It was like riding a never-stopping roller coaster. This was going to be great! It was after lunch however, when we were hit. Like dominoes falling in a row, we all tumbled into our beds, holding our stomachs. Everything we had eaten that day came up. Only Jim seemed unaffected by it. The rest of us were undoubtedly—seasick!

We called for the steward and told him our problem. We begged him to bring us something to help. He appeared at our door shortly with a tray of cheese, crackers and oranges. This combination had been known to help settle upset, seasick stomachs, he informed us. We lunged at the tray and consumed what we could coax our reluctant mouths to swallow. Then each retreated to his bed, hoping the worst was past. The cheese, crackers and oranges made their appearance again however, but this time not on the tray. It was like feeling your stomach was about to drop out of your body, and wishing it would too!

In fact, we had once heard a good description of seasickness from a friend. He had said, "When you first become seasick you're afraid you're going to die—then you get to feeling so terrible you're afraid you won't die—and that thought is even worse!" How fitting that was. We lay in our bunks moaning!

That's when Betty delivered her low blow. "Norm, I thought you told the travel agent we were bringing our own Doctor along with us! Why don't you do something about getting Him here?"

I must admit I felt half-provoked at her. After all, she could pray as well as I could—and at the moment I felt so sick I didn't even want to make the effort to pray, for myself or for anyone else. I turned over in bed and stared at the wall. It looked green, just like everything else in the room—including the rest of the family!

I started thinking. Or rather, the Lord started talking to me. It was as though He was gently reminding me of my position in this family. Jesus himself had placed me as the spiritual leader and I had a responsibility to fulfill that role. Betty's words pricked like darts in my mind. She was right. I had said those exact words. Now I was acting as though God, our great Physician, was back in New York somewhere. I guess most wives say things every once in a while that provoke their husbands. But every man has a choice whether to be stubborn and unyielding, or to take those words as a challenge and act upon the advice.

I decided to act. With a prayer for strength, I dragged myself out of bed and started crawling from one sick child to the next, laying my hands on them and praying that they would be well in Jesus' name. Betty wasn't too thrilled that I left her till last, but I did go to her too and repeated the same prayer. It was the Lord's problem then, not mine. He was "the Lord who heals" (Exod. 15:26 NIV). He was our Doctor, so He would have to come up with the cure. I crawled back into bed and pulled the covers around me.

By this time it was early evening—the ship was still tossing and so were we. But miraculously, one by one, we fell into a deep and peaceful sleep in the midst of that awful storm. All night we slept without any additional frantic dashes to the bathroom. In the morning we woke, feeling great! In fact, it was hard to imagine that we had been feeling so horrible the night before. It seemed just like a bad dream. We knew we had had a visit from our healing Father and He had touched each of us. How we praised and thanked Him for His goodness!

Other passengers suffered much longer than we did and there were far more turbulent storms in the next weeks. Nevertheless we all remained healthy for the remainder of the voyage, thanks to Jesus!

Twenty-three days on board ship seemed like a long time, although there were special little things that helped make the trip more exciting. For example, there was the time we saw the flying fish. They were so elegant and graceful. Once we spotted a porpoise. His comical antics were delightful! A small fire that broke out in our room one day didn't amount to much, but sure had the children excited for days. Little Marvin, one of the twins, would climb up on his bunk every day, look out the porthole and sigh. He really had us puzzled. We just couldn't figure out what he was looking at. Then finally one day, he climbed up, gazed out the tiny window and sighed in despair.

"Oh, no!" he groaned. "We haven't got up over that hill yet!"

We burst out laughing. We had never considered that the never-ending ocean horizon would appear like a far-off hill to a child. No wonder he was dismayed to think we weren't getting anywhere.

Despite the length of the voyage, it was a real treat to be together as a family for such a long period of time. Those three weeks were like another gift the Lord had given to us—a golden opportunity to share with each other and learn to know our children better. The insights we gained into their feelings on that trip would help us in the difficult weeks ahead when we all would be facing the trauma of adjusting to a new culture. Betty and I had lots of time for reflecting on how wonderfully the Lord had transformed our lives. We were able to discuss our hopes and hesitations about the future. We committed ourselves anew to God, to be used by Him in any way He would choose, in the land of Brazil.

Finally the long-awaited day arrived! We reached the port of Rio de Janeiro! Approaching the harbor, we could see the giant statue of Christ with outstretched arms, towering over the city. Sugar Loaf Mountain jutted straight up out of the water and seemed to be like a giant finger pointing to the sky. It was as if Jesus himself was there to welcome us and embrace us in this new land. We were overwhelmed with a sense of gratitude and urgency for our mission. We felt eager to win Brazilians to Jesus and help them learn to know Him as their real Friend.

Little did we realize we were soon to be jolted out of this lofty dream and hurled head-first into the nightmare of reality. In later years I was to learn the term "culture shock." In those first days and weeks in Brazil, I experienced it, though I had never heard the expression.

Within hours after we disembarked, we realized we were aliens. We could not communicate with anyone! It was like feeling we had been on a flying saucer and suddenly dumped on some strange, distant planet!

Some missionary friends did their best to help us get settled. We made a couple of moves in the first week, until we found a house large enough to accomodate our seven-member family. Then we were on our own.

I discovered quickly I had to become a good pantomime artist. It was either that or starve. When I would run down to the corner store, what would have been a ten-minute jaunt in the United States, became an hour-long drama. The difficulty arose from the fact that in those days, most items were kept behind the counter in Brazilian stores. You could not pick items off the shelf, although even that would have been hard for me since I could not read the labels anyway! I was forced to act out every grocery item we needed. It always made me feel rather silly going through my routine, but when the day came that I had to act out "toilet paper," I was absolutely humiliated! There were some items on Betty's list which I never purchased, because I just couldn't communicate. And Betty was too timid to even try.

We went to church, eager to get our first taste of a Brazilian service. We could not recognize even one word. We sat for nearly two hours on hard benches, straining desperately to hear some familiar sound—nothing! How were we ever to share Jesus' love when we could not understand or speak one word of Portuguese?

The children went through their own personal language crises. The twins, being the youngest, and not yet old enough to start school, faced a neighborhood of strange children. In their uninhibited enthusiasm, however, they managed to work out simple forms of communication. After just a short time, I was amazed to observe them playing happily with the Brazilian children. What was so puzzling to me was that our boys would speak in English to the Brazilians, and their playmates would respond in Portuguese. Somehow they understood each other even though they were speaking two different languages. I wished it could be so easy for us adults!

The older children had a more difficult time. Since we could not afford the high-priced American school, we had no alternative but to enroll our children in a Brazilian school. I pitied them as I watched them trudge down the street that first morning on their way to school. When they returned that afternoon, I could tell from the droop of their shoulders and downcast eyes, it had not been an easy day for them. The missionary's boy who was to escort them to the school and introduce them to their teachers had deserted them in the schoolyard, leaving them to fend for themselves. Joann, aged thirteen, and Jim, aged eleven, had been placed in second grade. Their humiliation was written all over their faces as they told me about it. Eight-year-old Johnny did not seem to mind too much that he had been placed back in first grade, but the age difference was not quite so obvious for him as it was for his older brother and sister.

As the months went by however, the boys did their best to adjust and with the quickness of children were soon speaking much better than their parents. It was Joann who worried us most. In the U.S. she had been an excellent student—now she was being forced to study with second graders. The embarrassment came to the place of being unbearable for her. Each day she would return in tears! It was as though she had convinced herself it would be impossible to learn the new language. We prayed and tried to encourage her, but nothing seemed to help.

One day Joann once again broke into tears. She ran into her room, slammed the door and collapsed across the bed sobbing. We did not know how to console her. We felt the strain of learning a new language too, but at least Betty and I could comfort and support each other. The boys too could stick together. But Joann, more than anyone, was on her own!

Finally we decided to let her stop school and made plans for her to start studying through American correspondence courses. With greater desperation than ever, we committed this whole situation to Jesus. He had healed our children physically; surely He could heal them emotionally as well. It would have to be supernatural help now, because she had given up trying. We claimed a mental healing for her. We began thanking Him for solving the problem.

The change was not instantaneous, but within just a few days we noticed a marked improvement in Joann's attitude. She seemed so much more cheerful and interested in what was going on. Later that week I was out on the street trying to converse with some neighbors. Joann came along and stood there listening. It suddenly dawned on us both that she had been understanding the conversation! I felt like shouting! She was over the hurdle and on her way to learning Portuguese!

From that moment on, Joann's attitude toward Brazil and the people began to change. She became more confident and in a short time was speaking as well, if not better than the rest of us! In future years Joann became very close to Brazilian people. She roomed at Bible school with Brazilian girls and eventually fell in love with and married a Brazilian pastor.

Her miraculous adjustment to the language and culture was a blessing and inspiration to us all!

Shortly after Joann's language crisis passed we received a letter from the Stanley Martin family, our good friends in Pennsylvania. The letter asked us how Joann was doing. They had felt extremely burdened for her during those weeks of language struggle. They had prayed fervently. Not even knowing the situation she was facing, they had been impressed with the need to pray for Joann. I learned an important lesson from this whole experience.

Sometimes we get to thinking we have some foolproof formula, or corner on God. We get to thinking that our prayers are extraspecial. I realized in a new way that we need to really pray for each other. Of course the Lord had heard our prayers for Joann and He had heard Joann's prayers too! But when I learned of the intercession the Martin family had made for our daughter, it dawned on me forcefully that within God's family, we need each other! I was thrilled to see God's goodness poured out on us though we in no way merited it. After all, it was God's Holy Spirit, not us, who impressed upon that family the heartache Joann was suffering. Again, it was God who cared most! Praise His name!

Betty and I struggled with the new language too, of course, but somehow the strong sense of mission we felt, carried us through the hard times.

At language school we were the oldest couple, and the couple with the least education. What came easily to the other missionaries was an ordeal for us. To add to our self-consciousness, we had no idea what we were going to do when our language course was completed. Every other couple in school was with some mission board or denomination and had a good idea of what their assignment would be. We had absolutely no notion of where we would be going, and it was embarrassing to admit this to the other missionary students.

Despite our efforts, private tutoring help and earnest prayers, we were forever saying the wrong things. I would say, "thank you" when I meant to say "hello." Betty would say "see you later" instead of "excuse me." When a Brazilian neighbor of ours got burned very badly we couldn't even express our concern to his family. We did go over to their house and pray for him in English. It seemed a very meager gesture, but we desperately wanted to show them that Jesus loved them and that we loved them, in spite of the language barrier.

We just about had reached the point of despair in our studies! The other students were doing so much better than we were. Once, however, a teacher shared a very challenging thought with us—she said that the "language of love communicates the most." We thought about this a lot. One thing was certain, we did love the people. Ever since Jesus had transformed our lives, we were filled with a burning desire to communicate His love to others. The Brazilians had a different language, a different environment and some different customs, but they were real people just like us, with real problems. And we knew the Savior who could help them. We determined to do our best at learning the language and then trust the Lord to make up for lack of fluency, by channeling His love through us to those around us. We became excited about the ministry He would give us!

There was still one big question in our minds. What was that ministry going to be? We knew very little about the huge country of Brazil and even less about where our ministry would be most needed. It continued to be embarrassing to listen to the other language school students talking about their assignments. They all seemed to have such a clear idea of what lay before them. I am sure they judged us as being rather ignorant and a bit naive in that we had not planned ahead more. It was just one more thing we had to commit to the Lord. We were reassured that when the time came He would lead us clearly.

One day during the last weeks of language school, a teacher called us into her office. Having heard of our dilemma, she had a suggestion. There was a town she knew of, called Tabatinga, which had some Christians in it, but no pastors or missionaries. She had a sincere burden and concern for the believers there. The more she shared, the more our interest grew. Before we left her office that day, we had the name and address of one of the believers in that town. We were already eagerly making plans to visit there the following weekend.

When the weekend arrived, we waited impatiently for Lester Ebersole to arrive. He was going to drive us to the town, since we had no car of our own. When he finally pulled up at the house, all seven of us scrambled into his vehicle, anxious to reach our destination. The four-hour trip was fun—full of singing, laughing and imagining what might be in store for us in Tabatinga. Would this be our new home? We could hardly wait to get there!

Then came my big discovery! Just as we were about to enter the town, I reached in my pocket for the paper with the name and address of the contact person. "I must have put it in my other pocket," I thought nervously, and began fumbling in my other pockets. I got a sinking feeling in the pit of my stomach! Could I have forgotten the paper? I nudged Betty and whispered the problem to her. Perhaps by some miraculous chance, she had the paper in her purse. She looked at me in horrified disbelief and began searching frantically through her pocketbook. She found nothing.

As the realization dawned upon everyone that we had no way of knowing where to go in the town, a groan swept through the car. Tabatinga was a fair-sized town of about three thousand people. It could take us a couple of days to knock on doors asking for the person on the paper. And that would not help anyway, since I had forgotten what his name was too! I could have kicked myself, and the disgusted glares I was getting from everyone else in the car were just about as good as a kick too!

It was Lester who came up with the first reasonable suggestion.

"Look," he said matter-of-factly, "it's too bad that we don't have the name or address, but the Lord knows Norm didn't do this on purpose. It was just a mistake. Anyone can make mistakes. But we need help now, so let's stop complaining and throwing blame and pray about it!"

That made sense! By this time we were in the town. Lester stopped the car. Right there, we simply asked the Lord to forgive me for my carelessness and to guide us to this family, and make the trip worthwhile in spite of my mistake. We thanked Him for helping us! With an "Amen" that echoed through the car, we glanced at the neighborhood in which we were parked.

It was obviously not a residential section, so Lester started the engine and began driving through the city once more.

After a few minutes we had arrived at the top of a high hill and could look down on much of the town below us. Lester stopped the car in front of one of the houses.

"Let's just ask at this house if they know of any crentes (believers) in town," he suggested. So we headed up to the gate. Lester clapped his hands as is the customary Brazilian way of knocking. A lady soon appeared, wiping her wet hands on her apron. "Hello, how are you today?" Lester began in the polite way Brazilians were used to. I wished he would hurry and get to the point. "I was wondering if you could help us. We are looking for some people who call themselves crentes. Have you ever heard of any people like that in this town?"

The lady finished drying her hands and nodded. With a quick sweep, she pointed to the house next-door. "There are some crentes in that house," she offered simply. "Why not ask there? Maybe they know the people you're looking for."

"Thank you so much! We'll do that! Bye!" Lester about dragged us along. I felt like running too! The excitement I often felt, when I realized God had just done something extra special for us was mounting in my chest. I muttered a "Well, praise the Lord!" and followed Lester. "Imagine," I thought to myself, "the Lord could have left us floundering here all day—after all, it was my fault we didn't have the address—but in spite of all that, He led us to Christians at the house next door. Isn't He good?" I sang out, "Glory to the Lord! O give thanks unto the Lord for His goodness!"

By this time all the children had tumbled out of the car, joining us at the gate of the house next door. We clapped and waited expectantly. In a moment a young girl appeared—a teenager dressed very neatly and with a shy smile on her face. "Good day, may I help you?" she asked bashfully.

Lester began to explain. He told her how Betty and I and the children were American missionaries.

And that was about as far as he got. He had scarcely finished the word "missionaries" when she turned and fled into the house. We were puzzled, very puzzled. Brazilians are characteristically friendly and polite. To leave guests standing on the street was considered very rude, yet the girl had not seemed like the rude type. We kept standing there, wondering what to do.

We reasoned that maybe she was just too shy, especially since we were Americans, and that she had gone to call someone else.

A moment later, the girl reappeared with a lady we assumed to be her mother. They were both wearing huge grins. They threw open the gate and ushered us up the walk and into their house, as if we were some long-lost relatives! Frankly, it seemed more mysterious all the time. Soon the story poured out. It was still kind of hard for Betty and me to understand Portuguese, especially when people started talking really fast. So we had to strain to catch what they were saying. Both mother and daughter were so excited they just chattered on without a break.

Gradually we grasped what they were saying. The teen-aged daughter was just home from school for Easter vacation. That very afternoon the other Christians from the town had gathered in their living room for prayer. There was a single purpose for the prayer meeting. They were asking the Lord to send missionaries to their town. They had pleaded and rea-soned with the Lord, saying, "Lord, the missionaries always go to the big cities, but we need help too! Please, Lord, send someone here to teach us more about following you!" When we arrived at their gate, announcing that we were missionaries, the girl was so thrilled, she had forgotten her manners and ran to give the news to her mother.

"Mother, they're here! They're here!" she cried.

"Who's here?"

"The missionaries we prayed for!"

We felt a little like Peter must have felt when Rhoda left him standing at the door and ran with the good news to the praying people inside the house (Acts 12:12-16).

As we continued conversing with the girl and her mother, I had a growing sense of peace and gratitude in my heart. This was where the Lord wanted us to work. He had done it again! His goodness was overwhelming! By the time we left Tabatinga that day, we had met several other believers in the town. They embraced us warmly and we knew we would have a sense of "belonging" here. Some of the folks had heard of a house for sale. We went and looked at it. It would be just great for our needs! Within a few hours we made the necessary arrangements to reserve the house.

As we returned to our home in the big city of Campinas, and resumed our language studies, we couldn't contain our excitement. The Lord had led us again! Before we had even called, He had answered us (Isa. 65:24). How glad we were that our lives were in His hands!

Six weeks after our visit to Tabatinga, our studies were completed and we moved to our new home. We were loaded down with our own belongings plus scores of gifts received at a surprise shower given in our honor by fellow missionaries. We felt like newlyweds about to set up housekeeping!

All the children pitched in to help us unpack! They were so cooperative and enthusiastic about their new home. I can still picture Jim, cleaning around the fruit trees in our yard and even busily organizing our closets and drawers for us. We were home!

It was the realization of a dream and yet just the start of another great adventure. We had come to see, through our days of adjustment to Brazil, that our Lord doesn't always spare us from the difficult and strenuous learning experiences. However He does give us the strength to face them and joy in the midst of them. Along with the trials, He had showered upon us so many delightful little (and big) surprises that life was truly a satisfying experience. We didn't have any idea what the years ahead would hold, but we rejoiced that we would live them with our loving Creator!

7

Tabatinga

The years we spent in Brazil were eventful, to say the least! It would take another book just to tell all that the Lord did for us during that time!

Some of the highlights are unforgettable—like the first church service we conducted in Tabatinga.

We had just moved in, fresh out of language school and still rather unsure of ourselves. Betty and I had discussed our plan of action at some length. We would settle down in the community, visit some of the neighbors and maybe in a month or so, start holding some small weekly meeting. That didn't seem too threatening.

The Brazilians had a different idea. The Christians in that town had been waiting a long time for a pastor and they weren't about to wait any longer. One of them showed up at our house while we were still unpacking and announced calmly that he would be back on Sunday morning for the service. We were terrified and tried to let him know we wouldn't be having a service then, but we did not succeed at getting the message across.

114

About fifty people showed up on Sunday. They were quite a mixture—a Methodist family, a Presbyterian, a Lutheran, a Baptist and even an American family that had settled in Brazil. We had no choice but to hold a service. Betty told a Bible story and gave a brief testimony. I stumbled through a short sermon. We led in some songs and closed the meeting in prayer. We were pretty shaky—after all we had never spoken so much Portuguese all at one time. It was exhausting! We found out later that in one of our songs we had been singing that Jesus would cut all our heads off, instead of put a crown on our heads. It was embarrassing! Yet the people were so gracious and accepting. We felt encouraged that in spite of our mistakes, the Lord was going to do some very wonderful things in Tabatinga. We determined to preach only "Jesus Christ as Lord and ourselves as merely His servants" (2 Cor. 4:5, 6). He would have to show others that the power we had received was from God and not our own.

About two weeks after we had settled in Tabatinga, a man came to our door.

"Is it true? Do you believe your God heals?" he asked gruffly.

"Yes, we do!" I answered with enthusiasm. We certainly had had more than enough personal experience to prove that.

"Well, you should visit Eduardo. His son is very sick!"

I asked the visitor for directions to Eduardo's house and promised to stop there as soon as possible. He thanked me and left.

When Betty and I arrived at the simple country hut, we were met outside by Eduardo. His son was very ill, he explained. They had been to many doctors and none could help him. Could we do anything for him, he pleaded desperately.

I accompanied this nervous father into the dark house, where the boy lay listless on a small cot. He looked to be about ten years old. He had a large lump on his thigh and was burning with fever. I did not have to be a doctor to know this was serious.

Without hesitating, I laid my hands on this child and began to pray. I had learned we don't have to be great orators to come to God. I simply asked Him to heal this little boy, in Jesus' name, and then thanked Him for doing it. I turned to the father and told him what I was already sensing in my heart—God would heal his son. The promise of John 15:16 was reliable. It said, "Whatsoever ye shall ask of the Father in my name, He will give it you."

The dad looked at me a little skeptically, but I could see a familiar glimmer of hope in his eyes. In his own way, he was reaching out in faith too. He was trying to believe with me that God had healed his boy. There was a lighter spring to his step as he walked with me out to our car, and the hopelessness was gone from his voice as he thanked me and waved goodbye.

I wondered if I would ever see them again.

I did not have to wait long. The very next day I looked up from my work to see a horse and rider approaching our house. I watched with curiosity and then surprise as I recognized the rider to be the 10-year-old boy for whom I had prayed.

The anticipation mounted inside me as I hurried out to meet him. The little fellow jumped off his horse with ease. He wore a broad grin and seemed to be brimming with energy. There was little similarity between this child and the suffering one we had visited the previous day.

It didn't take more than a minute till he had made his triumphant announcement. "This Jesus you prayed to, healed me!" His smile was radiant! God had healed him! I glanced at his leg. It was the same size as the other one. The lump was gone. Another glance at his beaming face assured me that this boy was just as healthy as could be.

"Well, praise the Lord! Thank you, Jesus!" I exclaimed, giving the boy an affectionate hug. Our Lord had done it again! Though I had already seen so many miracles of healing, each new one just overwhelmed me with a sense of wonder at the power and love of God! I thought of the verse in Lamentations which says, "Great is thy faithfulness . . . Thy mercies are new every morning!" (Lam. 3:22, 23). How true! I just had to shake my head in amazement and laugh with delight at the supernatural power I had just seen displayed again!

The boy was just as elated as I was! He rushed on in a tumble of words, telling me how good he felt—how he was able to play with his friends again—how he knew it was God who had healed him. I invited him to stay for a while, but he was impatient to be off.

I understood. There were other people he wanted to see and he was bubbling with the desire to share his good news. Before he rode off, he turned and called back to me.

"Oh, I almost forgot," he shouted, "we'll be seeing you at church on Sunday! My mother wants to learn more about your God!" And with that he trotted off down the road.

To be honest, when I prayed with that father and son, I really had not thought about them as possible "church members." God had impressed upon us the importance of each individual, no matter how simple or poor they seemed to be. We had come to be not so concerned about whether people attended "our church," but about whether they knew our God—the God of the universe—the God who showed His tender and compassionate love by sending Jesus to this world to die for sinners.

I realized my motive in praying for this boy had been a simple one of concern for his physical and spiritual well-being, and not one of "proselytizing." Nevertheless, his parting statement thrilled me. I looked forward to being able to share more about the love of Jesus, with this child and his family. I prayed that each one of his family would come to know our Savior as their own personal Friend.

Betty and I continued to pray for them throughout the week. When Sunday rolled around we prepared excitedly for the culto (Portuguese for "service"). The people began to arrive and the living room was filling up fast. In a moment, Betty nudged me and pointed out the window. A wagon had just creaked to a stop at the gate. Our little friend was sitting happily up front with a woman we guessed to be his mother. In the back of the wagon were three other boys who looked like various-sized duplicates of the ten-year·old. Seems we would have a chance to know more of this family.

We greeted them warmly. The mother's name was Joanna. She clasped our hands and thanked us for our prayers. She gave a loving hug to her son who had been healed, and shuffled shyly over to one of the chairs we had set up for the congregation.

The meeting went fairly well that day. We were amazed to sense the people responding to God's Word, in spite of our poor pronunciation and grammatical errors. We were humbled at the thought of how God could use just ordinary people as His instruments!

When Joanna accepted Jesus as Savior and Lord of her life, and received the power of the Holy Spirit as well, our hearts were filled with joy. Soon after, she led her husband, Eduardo, and many of her relatives and neighbors to the Lord also. This family became pillars of the church. Later, we were surprised to discover that Joanna had been the leader of the spiritists (Satan-worshipers) in that town. Though extremely influential, all her powers had been unsuccessful in healing her son. It was Jesus' power and love which now won her devotion.

As our time in Tabatinga increased, our admiration for our God who is "no respecter of persons" (Acts 10:34) increased too. A poor, little old grandmother started attending our meetings. She was anxious to share her story with us.

She had worked as a maid for a rich family some years before. One day an ad in a newspaper, discarded by the family, caught her eye. It advertised a Bible. Some spark of interest was kindled in her though she had never before heard of the Bible. In simplicity she talked to God and told Him she wanted a Bible. When she came to our meeting she shared

119

her desire with us. We would gladly have given her a Bible, but she had told God she would work for it. She insisted on keeping her promise to God. Little by little her savings grew until she finally was able to purchase the much-desired Book. She returned to our home, joyously clutching her new Bible.

"Now you must pray for my eyes so I can read my Bible," she stated matter-of-factly.

We were astonished to learn that this lady had sacrificed so much in order to buy a Bible she could not even read. Her eyesight was terrible. Even her glasses did not help.

Nevertheless, we prayed. God knew this lady's sincerity and He cared for and loved her. Surely it would be His will for her to be able to read His Word and learn more about the One who had created her. As was our habit, we just gave the problem to the Lord and thanked Him for working it all out. Then we quit worrying about it.

Very little time passed before this tiny lady was back at our house. Her eyes had improved miraculously and she now was able to read her treasured Bible. In fact, she was not only reading the Word, but memorizing it too. Before long she had memorized over forty Scripture verses. This humble little grandmother who had hardly any schooling was now teaching others the Word of God which she had hidden in her heart. How true the Scripture is which says, "God has chosen the foolish things of this world, to confound the wisdom of the wise" (1 Cor. 1:27). We marveled at the way He operates!

The tiny congregation in Tabatinga grew. Before long we were able to rent a building which provided us with more space. The people were hungry for spiritual truth and as God promises, "Blessed are those who hunger and thirst after righteousness for they shall be filled" (Matt. 5:6). It thrilled us to see people, one by one, becoming rooted and grounded in God's Word and sharing Jesus with their friends and relatives.

Two and a half years seemed to fly by. We were thoroughly enjoying the work to which God had called us. We were surprised and a bit confused then, when we received an invitation to move to another state in Brazil to manage a large coffee farm owned by an evangelical mission board.

Our first reaction was to disregard the request. After all, who would take over the work in Tabatinga? It was just getting firmly established—to leave at this point would be unfair. However, the thought of living on a farm again was appealing. Having always loved life on a farm, it would be challenging to take on such a large coffee farm. At the same time we would be responsible for pastoring a church located on the farm and ministering to the twenty or more families who lived there also. The purpose of this farm was to provide both spiritual and financial help to the families. Each worker was leased a plot of land for four years. If he prospered, he could buy his own piece of land in the jungle, clear it, build a hut and evangelize that area. That sounded like a worthwhile missionary project.

The weeks went by and I was feeling increasingly uneasy. Slowly I realized it was the same feeling I had when the Lord first spoke to me about going to Brazil. Could it be that He really wanted us to take the farm job?

Betty and I began to pray seriously about the matter. We decided we would leave it up to the Lord to show us very clearly what to do. A replacement for the Tabatinga church was an absolute must, so we told the Lord if He wanted us on the farm, He would have to supply someone to take our place.

We quit worrying about it and left the whole situation with Jesus. We did however, write a letter to our friends, the Ebersoles. At that time, they were in the United States on furlough. We asked them to pray with us.

Letters must have crossed in the mail because shortly after mailing our letter to the Ebersoles, we received one from them. We were amazed! Their letter asked us to pray with them because they had felt led of the Lord to leave the city in which they had been working. Another missionary had already taken over their responsibilities for them. Lester and Lois were in the process of seeking the Lord's will concerning a new place of ministry in Brazil. "Did we know of any place needing a pastor?" they wrote.

We were convinced this letter from them was also God's answer to us concerning the farm. The Ebersoles would make ideal replacements in Tabatinga!

We prayed with them about it a little longer and were absolutely at peace that this was the right decision. The parting from our friends in Tabatinga was difficult of course, but knowing that God was leading us gave us a calmness and inner joy beyond comprehension.

The mission board which owned the coffee farm in the state of Paraná was called the United Missionary Church. They requested that we take a furlough before going to the farm. It wasn't too hard to persuade us to cooperate with that idea! The Lord was so good! Here we had gone to Brazil, never expecting to see our American friends and loved ones again. Now, just three and a half years later we would be able to visit with them. It made us feel very happy, excited and truly thankful!

The mission had offered to take on our support once we started work on Fazenda Peroba, as the coffee farm was named. That was an issue they wanted us to consider seriously during those furlough months.

The offer was tempting! We had lived by faith for over four years. God always took care of us and we did not suffer. We had been comfortable and happy. Still, it kept us on our knees. God's payments were never late, but they weren't often early either! "It might be nice to have a guaranteed income!" I reflected. One of our boys even urged, "Why don't we do it? Maybe we wouldn't have to pray so much—at least not for money!"

This would be security for my family. No one could accuse me of being worse than an infidel again! We could plan our budget more easily and even start saving again! I would not have to be so concerned about newsletters and correspondence with supporters so I could devote more time to the needs of the Brazilians.

All my arguments seemed reasonable enough to me, but they lacked one thing. Parroting them back to God each day gave me no peace. I would end up with a cold, empty feeling every time I did. Evidently God did not buy my arguments.

Finally I got desperate with Him! (You know, I believe we would spare ourselves a lot of heartache and misery if we would just decide to ask Him what He wants in the first place—instead of trying to persuade Him that we know best.)

"Lord," I prayed earnestly, "I think maybe you're trying to tell me we shouldn't take a salary from the mission. We've been living strictly on faith so far and you've always supplied all we needed plus much more. Thank you, Lord! But I need to know definitely that you want me to continue this way! So, Lord—well—I hope you won't mind, but I would like to put out another fleece."

At that point I had to think a little bit and decide what the fleece would be. I remembered a bill that had come that day in the amount of two hundred dollars. I did not have any money to pay it and in three days we were planning to leave for Florida. The bill needed to be paid before our trip. That would be the fleece.

"Jesus," I continued excitedly, "if you have someone send me enough money to pay this bill on time, then I'll know you want us to trust you for our income. If the money doesn't come in, then I'll know you want us to accept support from the mission. Thank you, Lord! I believe you're going to show us and whatever your answer is, I'll accept it gladly!"

Maybe God thought, "Here we go again!" But one thing about God—His patience is great!

Well, you probably guessed already. A check arrived in the mail, postmarked California, from someone I had met only once. The amount of the check was two hundred dollars. That was the answer!

I grinned, realizing the check had been in the mail, before I had even prayed. Isa. 65:24 echoed in my mind, "Before they call I will answer; while they are still speaking I will hear" (NIV).

I was delighted to carry out my part of the bargain! God had taken care of us all along. We had no reason to think He would forget about us now. As a family, we claimed Phil. 4:19, "Our God will supply all our needs according to His riches in Christ Jesus."

To Brazil and our new life on the coffee farm we went confidently—still trusting God to provide and knowing He would!

8

The Coffee Farm Classroom

Life on a Brazilian coffee farm was quite a bit different from life on a Lancaster County farm. I had always known farming was hard work and I had always been a hard worker. But at times it seemed to me that work on Fazenda Peroba was ten times harder than any I had ever done.

The jungle had been cleared by burning off the trees. What remained were large stumps and fallen logs scattered throughout the fields. Most of the planting had to be done by hand. To walk through the fields was like maneuvering through some sort of maze. I cringed sometimes when I imagined what some of my old farm buddies would say if they saw the crooked furrows and spotty crops.

The farm equipment was not in A-1 condition and when something broke (which seemed pretty often) we just could not run to the nearest hardware store to get a replacement part. The nearest store of any kind was at least twenty miles away, over dirt roads. Hardware stores were found only in the larger cities about forty miles away.

There was no pick-up and delivery system for our harvested crops. Whatever was ready to sell had to be hauled to the city of Maringa. That was some trip in those days! Dirt roads, washed out bridges, potholes and mud often slowed our journey by days!

It's impossible to remember how many all-night trips I made in an overloaded truck to sell the produce. Then I would drive all night back again to work! Some of those trips over muddy roads were hair-raising and more than once the brakes on our rickety truck gave out. Careening down the steep dirt roads, frequently I would call on the Lord for help. Only His protection kept us from serious accidents!

It was a hard life. But it was a lot of fun too! Our wooden house was large and cheery. A screened-in porch bordered three sides of it and we loved eating our meals out there. We could watch the beautiful South American sunsets, the palms swaying in the evening breeze and the warm, velvety darkness settling down across the fields each night.

There was something about our way of life there which forced us to draw closer to God. With no doctor for miles and no guaranteed support coming in, we had to rely on the Lord. We learned to depend on Him to help us do things we had never done before. He said, "My strength is made perfect in weakness" (2 Cor. 12:9). Repeatedly, we had to acknowledge how very weak we were. How we needed His strength!

For example, our son Marvin's mare had been gored by a mad bull. The boys came calling frantically for me to hurry and do something. When I reached the mare I shuddered. There was a big gaping hole in her side. Some of her internal organs were hanging out. My prayer life by that time was like second nature to me. I automatically whispered a prayer, "Help me, Jesus!" and started to work. I sent the boys for some nylon fishing line, pliers, a strong needle (the type we used for sewing coffee bags), alcohol and cotton. Then I began the gruesome task of pushing some of those organs back into her abdomen. When the boys returned panting from their errand, I did one of the crudest sewing jobs in history. There were several layers of tissue which needed to be repaired and horsehide is tough material through which to pull a needle. Finally I cut the last thread, wrapped a sack around her middle and secured it with a belt. I committed her to the Lord and asked Him to make her well. Then I turned away and staggered, almost passing out! A surgeon I was not! It was only Gods power that had gotten me through that gory mess!

The other farm workers did not share my faith. They declared firmly that there was absolutely no way the mare would live, and even if by some miracle she survived, she was sure to lose the colt she was carrying.

But that mare did not die. Her colt did not die either and she went on to bear other healthy offspring. The Lord had enabled me to do something with which I had had no prior experience, and in spite of my clumsiness, He performed a miracle. Praise Him!

I remember the day I burned my foot so badly. I had been working on the tractor, clearing logs from a section of land which had recently been burned off. The logs and underbrush were still smoldering and in spots the sandy soil was actually bubbling from the intense heat. I had to keep the tractor moving so it would not become overheated. All at once a log jammed the blade and the tractor was stuck! To leave it sitting there while calling for help would have meant losing the tractor. The tires would have caught on fire in no time and set the whole machine on fire. I had no choice but to work at freeing the blade myself. I jumped down and began tugging at the log. My feet sank down into the simmering soil, but I could not stop to think about what was happening to my own body. Within a few minutes I succeeded at loosening the blade. I leaped back up on the tractor and drove it out of the area onto cooler ground.

Then I painfully realized what had happened to me. My foot was burned badly. When I reached some of the other farm workers I could not get down from the tractor. The pain was mounting and it was impossible to put any weight on my foot. The men said I must have been crazy to have done what I did. Yet, I felt I had had no choice. Now I had no choice but to trust the Lord to do something about my foot.

I had never had much experience with burns, but as the men carried me into the house I felt strongly inclined to carry out a certain treatment, I told Betty to whip up lots of egg whites and plaster them on my foot. Putting my foot up to rest, I asked her to cover it with a plastic bag. My foot was not healed instantly, but the pain subsided rapidly and by the next morning I was walking on it. I knew the Holy Spirit had impressed on me a proper treatment and I praised Him for using that to bring about such a speedy recovery!

The Bible says, "Call on me and I will answer thee and show thee great and mighty things which thou knowest not" (Jer. 33:3). That's a tremendous promise and the Lord fulfilled it for us so many times!

Our years on the farm brought us closer to God through the example of the Brazilian people as well. Many times their deep spiritual hunger and simple faith served as models to us.

Often they decided to have all-night prayer meetings. As much as Betty and I liked to pray, there were times when we wilted inside at the thought of staying up all night. Like most folks, we like our sleep. Nevertheless, we just could not turn the people down. They were hungry for more of the Lord and we certainly wanted to help them grow in their relationship with Him.

One night the youth group decided to pray all night. Up until that time, the young people of the church seemed to be more interested in playing games and enjoying social times than praying. So we were encouraged with this new desire for prayer.

Nothing out of the ordinary happened that night. It was just a peaceful evening. We were pleased to hear the youth seeking God. Still, nothing spectacular occurred.

However, on a Sunday evening not long afterward, we saw the results of that night of prayer. As I preached that Sunday, about the dry bones mentioned in Ezekiel, I could feel the Spirit of the Lord hovering over the entire place. As God breathed life into those old bones, He began breathing new life into all of us. People began to weep. Many went to others asking forgiveness for wrongs they had committed. Some were laughing with delight. One woman who could neither read nor write, began singing in a beautiful heavenly language—a song of worship to the Lord. The lay pastor who assisted me was usually a very vocal, outgoing sort of man. That evening, however, he moved with a strange quietness and gentleness among the congregation, laying hands on various people and praying that they would receive the baptism of the Holy Spirit.

That evening was especially sweet for all of us. It proved to be no mere passing emotional experience, for it resulted in many permanent changes. Families were drawn closer together, individual lives were transformed. Our young people started to go out two by two, to witness. Some of these folks are still working for the Lord today in Brazil.

For a long time there were no more sack races at youth meeting. Everyone was just so eager to study the Bible and pray and help others that the social times became much less appealing. We recalled the verse in Acts which says, "After they prayed, the place where they were meeting was shaken. And they were all filled with the Holy Spirit and spoke the Word of God boldly" (Acts 4:31 NIV).

When our sons, Mervin and Marvin, returned from the mission boarding school, they attended one of the youth meetings. It lasted four hours, yet when they arrived home later, they unashamedly admitted they had not been bored! God was working!

It was impressive to see how God had miraculously entered the lives of these simple farm folk! And it was not because of anything we had done or said, but because of their desire to know Him, and because of His impartial love for individuals. We became convinced more than ever that those who search for God with their whole hearts will find Him (Jer. 29:13).

It was beautiful to observe many of these Brazilian Christians learning to trust God for their everyday needs. As they trusted Him for small daily problems, their faith grew to trust Him for bigger things too! We were especially thankful for this one day when we ourselves were in dire need of their prayers!

I had been out working in the garage. We were expecting company soon so Betty was back at the house, getting things cleaned up in preparation for our guests. I knew she was planning a major project that afternoon, but it really did not concern me much.

Several months before, Betty had painted the cement floor in our kitchen. For some reason the paint never dried properly and every time we walked across it we felt like flies must feel on tar paper. Betty certainly did not want our visitors to have to put up with the mess, so she decided to remove the paint.

Someone had told us that gasoline would do the trick, so that afternoon Betty tackled the task of removing the sticky paint with gasoline.

She knew it was a dangerous thing to be working with and she tried to be very careful. Unfortunately, in her haste to get the job completed, she knocked over the jug of gasoline and it spilled across the floor. Moving quickly to sop it up with rags, she forgot one critical fact. Our refrigerator was powered by kerosene, with a pilot light burning constantly.

When the gas fumes reached that flame, the kitchen exploded! Out in the garage I heard a roar like thunder. I turned to see flames pouring out of the kitchen windows and door. For a few agonizing moments I thought Betty must have been killed and, from all appearances, it looked like the whole house would be gone too!

I raced to the house, praying as I ran. As I drew closer, I was relieved to see Betty outside. Her skirt was burned off and I knew she must be hurt pretty bad, but she was alive. She was frantically motioning for me to do something about the house. So I turned my attention there.

A few men who had witnessed the scene, helped me in grabbing containers, filling them with water from the laundry tubs and then carefully dousing the flames. In a few minutes the fire was out.

Amazingly, there was not much damage to the house. It was Betty who had suffered the most. Her legs and feet were burned badly. No egg white mixture was going to be sufficient for burns like these. We carried her gingerly into the house and let her sit in a tub of cold water. I prayed, Betty prayed, the family prayed. Yet the pain continued. It was all she could do to keep from screaming. The tears streamed down her face.

In no time news of the accident spread among the farm families and people began calling at our door to ask about Betty. Many of them would only be content if they could see her for themselves, and thus began a line of spectators, filing through our bathroom to get a glimpse of Betty. They had to reassure themselves that she was really alive.

Many of them wept. Many gave advice. And many prayed. All were so sorry for their dear "Dona Betty." Finally, one little woman came. Her name was Jovalina. She was a simple country person, but more than anyone, she seemed to be able to feel with Betty. Her tears were not so much tears of pity, as tears of experience.

"Oh, Dona Betty," she cried. "So many times you have prayed for us. You and Norman have prayed for our sick and they have recovered. You have prayed for our young people and they have begun to serve Jesus. You have prayed for our families and they are happy now. Now it is our turn to pray for you. Now you are suffering. Now it is time for us to bear the burden for you."

Then she prayed. Simply, humbly and beautifully, she prayed that the Lord would help Betty to be well quickly. Betty could sense the depth and sincerity of Jovalina's desire. Through her own tears of agony, she realized this woman would have gladly undergone her suffering for her if only she could have. That was love! It was an example to us! Jesus' attitude had been just like that—willingness to suffer for each one of us whom He loved so dearly! How uplifting to see the love of Christ in that lady! We had to think of that verse in Philippians— "that I may know Him and the power of His resurrection and the fellowship of His suffering, being made conformable unto His death" (Phil. 3:10). Jesus suffered for us. We like to have His power, but rarely desire to share His suffering. Jovalina shared our suffering and in that way I believe she came to know Jesus in a more precious way. She had obeyed the command "Bear ye one another's burdens, and so fulfill the law of Christ" (Gal. 6:2).

Within a very short time Betty's pain had subsided. There were some hard days and a few scars remain to remind us of that accident. But her recovery was miraculously fast and we were all amazed at how good her skin looked afterward. No one would ever have guessed she had suffered second-degree and third-degree burns. That is the wonder of prayer, and that is the wonder of our Lord!

Some weeks later, we discovered that Betty's sister Edna had had some unusual dreams around the time of the fire. She became concerned about Betty and together with some other women prayed earnestly for her! How good God is!

Another startling answer to prayer came during that time on the farm. A woman who had been involved in witchcraft became a Christian and came to us with a problem.

"Pastor Norman, will you ask the Lord to give me a flock of chicks?" she pleaded.

I was surprised. "Don't you have any?"

She shook her head, "No, the ones I had got a disease and died!"

The logical thing was for her to buy a hen and eggs and start over, but this family was very poor. With eight or ten children, and not even enough money to buy proper food and clothing, this was impossible.

We had taught the people to believe the Lord would supply their needs and prosper them. But since this lady was a new Christian, we prayed for her, "Lord, please give this family a flock of chicks! Thank you, Jesus!"

She thanked us and returned home.

Soon afterward a hen came walking into her little hut. It strutted over to the corner of the room, in back of their home-made cookstove and laid an egg. The next day it returned and laid another one. After watching this for ten or twelve days,

Dona Anna said to her family, "I had better find out whose hen this is. It surely must belong to someone!"

So she picked it up and carried it to all her neighbors asking, "Is this yours?" After asking the last one, he replied, "Keep it! You've asked everyone, so now it's yours!"

She hurried home with the hen. It sat on the eggs and when they hatched she had the hen and little chicks for which we had prayed! Anna told everyone she met how God had given her that little flock—and we knew He did too!

We spent two three-year terms on the farm in Brazil. We were encouraged with the way the Lord blessed His Word there. The twenty-six families which were there when we began our job, had grown to forty families. All helped with the farm work. These families decided the little schoolhouse they had been using for worship was not large enough, and so they donated their time to construct a church building.

At Christmas time more than one thousand people came to our Christmas program. The farm families worked for hours in preparing a life-like presentation of the Christmas story, complete with horses and goats and a picturesque outdoor setting. It was a moving experience—one which made all of us focus our attention on the matchless love of God in sending His Son into this world for us.

The Lord gave us scores of delightful little surprises on Fazenda Peroba. For example, one day our twins begged Betty to make chocolate dumplings for them. Betty loved to please the children, but we had no eggs. The children had come to recognize how God's power operates.

"Why don't you pray for God to send us an egg? You pray about everything else, Mom!" they remarked. Betty looked a little startled at first and then seeing the obvious faith in the boys' eyes, she laughingly agreed. But she soon forgot about the prayer. When she saw a large bird atop a palm tree, she thought nothing of it. Even when the boys excitedly called her to come and see the egg they had found, the prayer did not enter her mind. Betty picked up the egg and examined it. There were no cracks! Then she remembered.

"How could this have fallen from that tree?" she wondered. The lowest limb was at least fifteen feet from the ground.

"Boys, maybe this is the answer to our prayer," she announced. They looked dubious. Marvin said, "Ugh, you wouldn't use a bird's egg to make food would you?"

Betty merely replied, "Let's take it in the house and break the shell."

They cracked the egg and into the bowl fell a perfect egg, with a large spotless yolk and thick white. "Thank you, Lord!" Betty rejoiced at God's interest in the small things of life. The Bible says God sees the sparrows that fall (Matt. 10:29-31), and He saw some young boys' desire for chocolate dumplings! He's a God who cares and—oh, I almost forgot—those dumplings were the best I ever tasted!

A missionary couple, Ray and Ethel Sahmel, came to visit us. Ethel was helping Betty prepare lunch when she suddenly spied a beautiful blue butterfly among the flowers. "Oh, Betty," she cried. "Could you get that for me? I have a butterfly collection at home."

Betty ran after the little insect, but with no net and her mind on her unfinished work, her effort was useless. She apologized, "Ethel, I'm sorry, but I couldn't get it."

"Oh, I wanted that so badly for my collection! They are gorgeous—those blue wings just glisten!" She seemed so disappointed. Betty began to wish she would have tried a little harder.

We had learned to pray about everything! The Lord said, "If we ask anything according to God's will He will do it" (1 John 5:14, 15 NIV). Sometimes we are sure what God's will is, but Betty could not be sure if it was God's will for Ethel to have that butterfly. After all, maybe it deserved its freedom. But then Betty remembered Ethel was her guest and we are told in the Bible to "offer hospitality" (1 Pet. 4:9 NIV), and try to please others (Rom. 15:2 NIV). So she suggested, "Ethel, all I know to do is pray about it!"

Propping the door open with a chair, she prayed, "Lord, I'm asking you to bring that butterfly in the kitchen. I don't have time to chase after it. Besides I couldn't catch it when I tried. So thank you, Lord, that you are going to bring it in!"

"It will come," she stated matter-of-factly to Ethel who was standing to the side, her mouth dropped open! It was the first time she had ever heard of anyone praying to catch a butterfly!

It seemed like the butterfly heard the prayer and did not want to get caught (who could blame it?) because it flew in the other direction. But Betty's faith had not given up. "The Lord will bring it back!" she assured Ethel.

That lovely butterfly circled and fluttered right back to the house, through the kitchen door and lighted on the counter top!

When Ethel returned to the city and told other missionaries, they wanted Betty to pray for more butterflies. They seemed to think she should get in the business! But we both realized there are far more important things to pray about than butterflies!

Nevertheless, it was a real lesson on faith to all of us. The God who knows how many hairs we have on our heads (Luke 12:7), cares about tiny details. He delights in giving good things to His children (Matt. 7:11).

Life on the Brazilian farm had become our way of life. We felt at home there. It was while there that the Lord brought two special little girls into our home. They became our daughters! How thankful we were that God had decided to give us the responsibility of caring for and loving Janete and Ivete. To them, we were the hope of a different and better future. To us, they were a spark of fun and liveliness and a very welcome addition to our family!

We were forced to admit however that our lives were changing. Joann had married Cleber, a graduate from the mission's Bible institute and they had blessed us with our first granddaughter. Jim had returned home to the United States in his late teens, married a lovely Christian girl, Charlotte Martin, and was settled in farm work back in Pennsylvania. The Lord was giving him his heart's desire. John was a student at Fort Wayne Bible College in Indiana. Our twins were ready for their last year of high school at the Missionary Church

Boarding School. Already, they were eagerly making plans for what they wanted to do after graduation. Janete and Ivete were the only children at home.

As much as we loved the people on the farm and life in Brazil, we began to feel restless. We wondered if God was trying to change our direction again.

It was a sudden sickness in the spring of 1971 which convinced us to return to the United States. Betty's mother had become very ill and was not expected to live. We decided this was the Lord's time for us to take a furlough. Because of Mother Wenger's serious condition, we felt Betty should return immediately to be with her mother. Our son-in-law Cleber and daughter Joann had decided to move to the U.S. for a period of time, so they would follow Betty by a few weeks, taking Janete and Ivete with them. I would stay on the farm to finish packing and wait for the twins who still had a few weeks left of their school term. Then we would fly back to join the rest of the family. After more discussion and prayer, a two-year furlough seemed wise. In this way Mervin and Marvin could complete their last year of high school in the U.S. and we could see them settled in a job or college before returning to Brazil. Plus, John would be graduating from college then too.

After Betty left, I began working on the necessary documents for the rest of the family to leave Brazil. It was a shock to discover a Brazilian law stating that children must be legally adopted for at least two years before they can leave the country. We had had our girls for much less time than that and I wondered how we would be able to get them home with us. I wrote to Betty, explaining the situation. Everywhere she went she asked people to pray and I did the same. Again the Lord answered! They were granted exit documents! At the end of May, Cleber and Joann, their daughter Sandy and our two daughters, Janete and Ivete, along with our pet parrot, flew back to the United States.

The twins and I joined them a month later. What would have been a joyous reunion was clouded by the news that my own father had died suddenly—just two weeks before I returned. Even in the midst of that sorrow, I sensed God's peace comforting and sustaining me!

Betty (who was not normally very business-minded) had found us a very nice house, rented it, furnished it and even had a job lined up for me. I was impressed again at how the Lord works things out so perfectly when you are following His plan. I had such peace, knowing that regardless of the obstacles, as long as we were following God's blueprints, He would miraculously take care of us!

Betty's mother did not die as the doctors had predicted. Her condition stabilized and there was even some slight improvement. She was well enough to come home from the hospital, but she would require a lot of care. After considerable prayer, we decided we would be willing to care for her. It was a different type of responsibility for us. Always used to a lifestyle where we could pretty much come and go as we pleased, now we were tied down. Yet it is in giving of ourselves that we receive. The Bible says, "In what measure you give it shall be given unto you" (Luke 6:38 TLB). This time was no exception. As we took care of Grandma, she improved and a whole new ministry opened up for us.

People began coming to our home for help. We had plenty of speaking engagements on weekends and through these contacts, people heard about what the Lord had done for us. It gave many hope that God could help them too. Thus, began a stream of callers, seeking to know God better.

We came face to face with a question we had never expected—whether or not to return to Brazil when the two years were up.

Grandma seemed stronger all the time. We had started reciting Philippians 4:7 with her. It says, "The peace of God shall keep your heart and your mind." Grandma became alert and talkative. She began to sing and pray again! She was a blessing! Yet living by herself was out of the question, and we just did not feel right about putting her in a nursing home. Our son Jim challenged us one day with a question that pricked our consciences. He said simply, "Why don't you write and ask your Brazilian friends what they would do in your situation?"

We did not have to ask! We knew what they would do. No matter how poor, or how overcrowded their living situation would be, the Brazilians never would neglect the elderly members of their family. We knew what their advice would be! I just committed the whole thing to the Lord and decided not to fret about it. He seemed to have impressed on us clearly that as long as Grandma remained as she was, our place was in the United States, carrying the responsibility of her care. If His plans changed in the future, I was sure He would show us plainly. I rested in my mind, confident that for the time being we were not to return to Brazil.

It took a little longer for Betty to become reconciled to the idea, however. I remember the day we took a long, wet walk in the rain discussing our feelings on the whole subject. Betty had been battling with herself, wondering if she wasn't secretly unwilling to return to South America. Finally, she gave up her own desires and became willing to resume the Brazilian work. It was at that point that the Lord gave her a deep peace which had been missing in her for months—it was the assurance that we were right to remain in Pennsylvania until such a time as He would show us otherwise. That was how I had been feeling for a long time, but how special it was that God had brought Betty to the same point of surrender. We walked hand-in-hand, the rain splashing on our faces, refreshed in our spirits, knowing we were one with each other and one with God's purpose.

At that point we had no idea God was using Betty's dear mother to prepare us for a ministry we never dreamed of. Romans 8:28 says, "All things work together for good to them who love God, to them who are called according to His purpose." God can take anything and turn it around for our good when we are loving and seeking to serve Him! Praise Him!

We looked back fondly on memories of Brazil and our friends there. We remembered with warmth and gratefulness how the Lord had invaded our lives and had changed all of us. But when we looked to the future, we wondered what He would lead us to next. Of one thing we were certain—He would keep on making our lives better and better, and that was a happy thought!

9

Abundant Living—Family Style!

Those years in Brazil had been so special to us! In the first years back in the United States we benefited often from the lessons God had taught us there. We had learned to depend on Him for just about everything—our health, our livelihood, protection and most of all for our happiness. We discovered that happiness is not dependent on circumstances—had that been true, we would have been pretty miserable people, because we had our share of problems. Instead, happiness depends on knowing that Jesus cares about us and is with us always! The Bible says, "When you pass through the waters, I will be with you!" (Isa. 43:2 NIV). No matter what difficulty came our way, we learned to say, "Thank you, Jesus! We know you're working everything out for our good because you love us!" It only made sense that the God who created us, also knew us best and loved us most! He knew exactly what situations would cause our faith to grow strong and our relationship with Him to mature. And do you know what? He never allowed us to go through more than we could endure (I Cor. 10:13). That's one of His promises! How could we lose when the Creator of the universe walked hand-in-hand with us through each day's events? Really knowing Jesus loved us was (and still is) the sweetest happiness we could have ever experienced!

Betty and I not only drew closer to God during those years in South America, but we grew closer to each other. With most of the children gone in our last years on the farm, we had more time to be alone together. We learned to share our hidden hopes, feelings and frustrations. We had to deal with temptations like any other couple. Sometimes there were hurts, misunderstandings—sometimes we were angry with each other or had wrong attitudes. But we learned to quickly humble ourselves, ask forgiveness—and remove ill will and bitterness, which remained inside us.

The better I learned to know Betty, the more I realized God had given me the wife who was perfectly suited to my needs. When I came in from the farm work, exhausted and tense, there she was with a smile, a giggle, a hug and a tantalizing treat on the table! When our schedule was abruptly interrupted by some crisis in a Brazilian's life, she was ready in a minute's notice to help! When I would want to settle for second-best, she challenged me to use my faith and believe God for the best! She was radiant and enthusiastic — adding sparkle and fun to an otherwise unemotional guy!

Our twins had bought used cars. Betty sometimes used Marvin's Javelin to run errands after we had returned to the U.S., because she had no other transportation when I was at work.

One day Marvin warned, "Mother, don't use my car anymore. It might let you set along the road. It's not working right."

So Betty followed his advice. However, one day she desperately needed a car. She decided she would trust God to make the car run okay and went to Marvin's room to hunt his key. Not finding it, she proceeded to my desk, where I kept several keys in one drawer. Grabbing one, she hurried out to try it in the ignition. Nothing happened, but "Thank you, Lord," she whispered and turned the key once more. The engine roared to life and Betty was off on her errand!

When Marvin came home from school she was busy making supper. "Oh, Marv, I used your car today!"

"No! You didn't, Mother!"

"Don't worry! Nothing happened. It worked just fine and I got home okay."

"But, Mother, you couldn't have used my car. I only have one set of keys and I took them to school in my jacket pocket. What key did you use?"

Betty pointed nonchalantly to my desk, "It's right there on top of your dad's desk!"

Marv picked it up and examined it, a perplexed frown creasing his forehead. When I returned from work later, he met me at the door. "Dad, what key is this?" He held it so I could see it clearly. One look at it and I knew immediately.

"Why, Marv, that's the key to our post office box in Brazil!"

"I don't believe this," he muttered and ran out to the Javelin. When he walked in the house later, he was shaking his head. "Dad, I'm going to hide this key! Mother could use my car any time she wants to with this!"

I just grinned and patted him on the shoulder. "Forget it, Marv. If your mother needs a car, she'll use any old key!"

I always marveled at the unpredictableness of life with Betty!

It was gratifying to know I complemented her life as well. Betty was impulsive and several times would have plunged blindly into some shaky venture. I was more cautious. Sometimes I had to put my foot down, and thereby I would save us from some predicament Betty may have gotten us into! She needed quiet strength for her life. A whirlwind of activity, she disliked slowing down or saying no. The Lord helped me be a steadying and calming influence in her life. Next to Jesus, I knew she looked to me for refuge and example. It was staggering to realize the responsibility I had as her spiritual leader. Ephesians says husbands should, "Love their wives as Christ loves the church" (Eph. 5:25).

I had to ask myself what that meant for me. How did Christ love the church? I've heard many men say He loved it by dying for it. If Betty's life were in danger, I would lay down my life gladly for her! However, sometimes it would be easier to die for her than to really live for her—like when I must lay aside my interests (reading the paper, working in the shop, etc.) in order to give her a needed hand. How did the Lord love the church? He was full of compassion, slow to anger, longsuffering, patient! He did not demand His own rights—did not live to please Himself. He was not a big boss, but a tender Shepherd—a leader not a driver! That's some standard!

Yet, as Betty and I grew closer to each other and to the Lord I noticed He was giving me a new sacrificial love for my wife. The responsibility I had once feared and shirked became a wonderful challenge and great satisfaction to me. It was the most important task God had given me and it felt rewarding to be fulfilling my orders as a Christian husband.

When we returned to the U.S. in 1971 it saddened us terribly to see so many marriages in trouble. We had grown up believing that only "very bad" people had bad marriages. So it was awhile until we could admit that now, even respected Christian people were separating and filing for divorce. When we ministered in churches or Bible studies, or at my job, we came face to face with people (very nice people too!) who were enduring a miserable marriage. There seemed to be such a need for teaching from God's Word for husbands and wives. Definitely the God that used marriage as an example of His relationship with His Church, could never take pleasure in watching such a relationship disintegrate. We began to study more to see what principles God had set down for husbands and wives. Our ministry at churches and organizations focused increasingly on the pattern God had designed for marriage.

We stressed that love is a decision—not a feeling! So many couples claimed that after years of marriage they did not love each other anymore because they did not feel anything for their partner. We challenged them to "act" like they were in love—by doing little deeds of kindness for each other and giving of themselves to help their mate! Real love would result from this kind of action! Real love, we affirmed, involved sacrificing oneself for the other's good!

Scores of hurting people began seeking us out for more specific kinds of counseling. All we could do was point them to the One who had answered our questions. We rejoiced to see couples discovering He could really save their marriages.

The phone rang often each day and the number of unexpected callers at our door increased. One evening, very late, I opened the door to greet a very dejected-looking man.

"You don't know me," he began, "but I heard you speak in Ohio. My wife just left me and our three children and has moved in with another man. I just don't know what to do!" He was distraught.

I invited Gary in to listen to his story, and he ended up staying the weekend with us. We took him along to a Bible study. It was at the home of a couple that had been divorced and then came back to God and were remarried. His hope was rekindled as he chatted with the host and hostess. Later, sitting around our kitchen table with the Bible between us, I challenged Gary to admit his own failure to God. We had observed that rarely is one person totally at fault in a problem marriage. He did ask the Lord to forgive him that night and resolved to return to his wife to ask her forgiveness as well. His attitude toward her changed to one of loving acceptance. He was obeying God's Word which says, "If you forgive men when they sin against you, your heavenly Father will also forgive you" (Matt. 6: 14 NIV).

Returning to Ohio, Gary located his wife at the other man's apartment, presented her with a fragrant bouquet of dazzling red roses, and humbly asked her to forgive him. Later she confessed that at the time she thought he must have gone crazy. Nevertheless it caused her to do some serious thinking.

That couple was reunited! They now have a wonderfully successful marriage and are encouraging others who are going through rough marital situations.

Not all marriages were falling apart as this one was. Some appeared relatively strong on the surface and yet there was no real joy and contentment. Betty was asked to go to the home of one such wife.

Carl and Jean loved each other. That was certain! However, Jean had been ill for much of their married life. She suffered from arthritis, asthma and other ailments for which she took a lot of medicine. She just could not be the kind of wife and mother she wanted to be. Each day her sickness made her weaker. However, she began studying the Bible and was fascinated to discover it talked about healing. Someone had given my wife's name to her, so she requested that Betty come and pray.

Walking into Jean's living room, Betty was not prepared for the sight that greeted her. She had expected to see some old lady, but this woman could only have been in her thirties. Immediately, she noted that at one time, Jean had been exceptionally attractive. Now, sitting on the sofa, with her house-coat wrapped securely around her, dark circles emphasizing her sunken eyes, she looked like someone who had come to the end of herself. In fact, she had already tried once to take her life but had not succeeded. Now she came right to the point.

"This won't take long," she stated simply. "I just want you to pray for me." Later Betty discovered that Jean had made a thorough study on the work of the Holy Spirit and healing. She was as ready as could be to receive a miracle. Betty prayed simply and felt the presence of the Lord unmistakably. She chatted a bit more and returned home.

The next morning our phone rang. Betty picked up the receiver to hear Jean's excited voice on the other end.

"I know I was baptized in the Holy Spirit yesterday, Betty! I was healed too! At least most of my symptoms are gone—but not all of them. Do we pray and ask the Lord again to heal me?"

"No, we just keep on thanking the Lord," Betty advised.

Then Jean asked if she should continue her medication. On that question, Betty would not commit herself. "That has to be your own decision, Jean," she stated emphatically. "No one else can or should make it for you."

"That's what Carl told me too," Jean replied thoughtfully.

"Well, I'll just have to pray about it some more." And she hung up.

The next time we saw Jean she was like a new person. She had asked the Lord what to do about her medication and it was as if a ticker tape running through her brain repeated, "I either healed you or I didn't—I either healed you or I didn't." Jean accepted the voice of the Lord, stopped her medication and experienced complete physical and emotional healing.

Immediately, her family noticed the change in her life and soon each one made a new commitment to the Lord too. She and Carl grew in closeness to each other and to the Lord. They were so eager to study the Bible and pray. Eventually they became missionaries to Haiti, and later were in full-time Christian ministry back in the U.S. They have a beautiful family and each member loves God and is growing in Him! "Nothing is impossible with God" (Luke 1:37 NTV).

We praised God that no problem is too hard or too big for Him. He has given us the assurance that His will is for families to be united, loving and serving Him. And He is able to cope with any hindrance, which is preventing that from happening—whether it is poor health, unfaithfulness, lack of communication, alcohol, drugs or whatever. He is able to work miracles if we are willing to give Him first place in our lives. It was thrilling to see how lives and marriages were being transformed by the power of God's Holy Spirit! We were so happy to be involved in the process!

When we had been back in the United States a couple of years, we decided to make a quick visit to Brazil. Our Brazilian friends were constantly on our minds. We figured a visit might encourage them and lift our spirits as well. The week before our departure was hectic — gifts to buy, packing to finish, plans to make for Grandma's care while we were gone, along with our already busy schedule of speaking engagements. We were exhausted and began dreading the idea of traveling. From experience, we knew we would get even less rest once we arrived in Brazil.

Ann Rowland, a friend of Betty's, came by to help with some last-minute preparations. Noticing how worn out we were she announced she was going to pray we would get a good rest before leaving.

Betty and I ruled that out as unlikely, although we appreciated her concern.

The day arrived and we rushed to the airport, only to be informed that our flight had been overbooked. Our initial reaction was dismay, until the airline agent explained we would be given free overnight lodging at the nearby Holiday Inn. Here was our needed rest! We praised the Lord! The next day we were able to leave feeling relaxed and refreshed and even a little richer, thanks to the cash we had received due to the "inconvenience" of the delay.

The month-long trip to Brazil was delightful! God's goodness never fails!

Upon returning, our lives settled into something of a pattern of irregularity and two more years sped by. There were always meetings at which to speak, Bible studies to attend, people to counsel on the phone, or searching people coming to our home for prayer. Besides all this, Betty continued to care for her mother and I worked a fifty-hour week as floor manager of Farmers' Supply Store in Lancaster. We felt fulfilled in the roles God had given us.

Our family scattered more during those years. Cleber and Joann and daughter Sandy had moved back to Brazil, followed a month later by John and his wife Sharon, and little girl, Monica. When they left, we realized how hard it must have been for our own parents when we first went to Brazil in 1960. Our son Jim, his wife Charlotte and children, Missy, Mike and Matthew lived not too far away. Marvin lived at home and had a good job in the town in which we lived. And of course our younger girls, Janete and Ivete, were attending the local high school. We enjoyed being close to these children and thanked the Lord for the joy they brought to us. However, Mervin was completing college studies in Indiana. We saw him occasionally, but never often enough it seemed. We missed him and the two families in Brazil. We prayed that someday we could all be together again!

Our longing to make yet another trip to Brazil increased. Now that part of our family was there, we felt a strong tug to visit them and see how they were doing.

As always, if something is the Lord's will, He will supply the finances. We were amazed that many people began giving us money for "your trip to Brazil," even before they knew we were actually planning such a trip. Before long, our fare was provided! In November 1976, we were on our way again!

What a joy it was to see our children and grandchildren after a year's separation. We laughed and cried and hugged and chattered all at once. What a surprise they had in store for us!

They had arranged for all of us to spend a week together in a cabin by the ocean. We anticipated a blissful week of relaxing on the beach, playing in the surf and catching up on lost time. We did not know it then, but that week was to mark the beginning of another dramatic change of direction for us.

One day while at the beach, Betty remained at the cottage while the rest of us went swimming. When we returned later that afternoon, Betty could hardly wait to get me alone. I knew she was anxious to tell me something, but I had no idea what it was. Finally, that evening we were by ourselves in our bedroom. The cottage was quiet and I was looking forward to lying there peacefully, soothed by the swishing of the tide and then dropping off into serene sleep!

But Betty had to talk—she began whispering excitedly!

"Norm, I've been so eager to talk to you alone! You know this afternoon when you all went to the beach and I stayed here? Well, while you were gone, the Lord gave me a vision!"

I squinted at her and raised up on one elbow. I had learned from experience that often in our relationship, the Lord had showed things to Betty before me. Sometimes the opposite was true. Nevertheless I had no desire to "tune out" the voice of the Lord if He had chosen to use Betty to speak to me. Now I wondered what it was that the Lord had shown to Betty and whether or not it would involve me. "Okay," I whispered back to her. "Tell me what He showed you!"

"I really wasn't expecting anything out-of-the-ordinary to happen this afternoon," she confided softly. "It was just such a gorgeous day and I was relaxing in the hammock, gazing up at the graceful palms and the perfect blue sky! I felt so close to the Lord—like I could have reached out and touched Him! Then it was just like my surroundings faded and events flashed into my mind. I felt like the Lord was revealing some things that would be happening to us." She paused for a moment, deep in thought.

"Go on," I urged. My interest was increasing rapidly.

"First of all, I felt He showed me there would definitely be a book written about all the Lord has done for us. But the strongest impression l got was that you would be quitting your job and that we would be involved in some sort of "full-time ministry" again. It was like the Lord showed me we would have a nice place in the country where people who need help and counseling could come and stay for a while. And guess what else? I saw that our children would be helping us in this work. Wouldn't that be wonderful!?"

When Betty made that last statement, the enthusiasm which had been mounting in me, drained away. Not that I didn't like the thought of having the children working with us. On the contrary, I loved the idea! But I just figured there was no way it could possibly happen. The children were settled in careers of their own and I certainly didn't want to be a meddling parent, trying to force them into a job they did not desire.

"Well, we will pray about it! But look, Betty," I warned sternly, "you'd better not mention this to anyone back home and we definitely don't want to try to convince the children. If it happens, fine. I'll be just as thrilled as you. But there's no way that I'm going to try to influence our children to do something like that. If it happens, we will know it was the Lord and not us who made it work out."

Betty was silent for a minute. "Yes, you're right, Norm," she conceded. "But I'm going to pray a lot and trust the Lord. The vision was so real, I'm positive it really is going to happen."

"Well, we will see," I murmured drowsily. "Good night, Dear." With that, I rolled over and went to sleep, leaving Betty awake, staring into the darkness, filled with warm thoughts of what might be.

Upon returning to the United States, we remained true to our plan and kept the vision to ourselves for a long time. During that time our schedule became busier each month with people coming for personal counseling and our constant itinerary of speaking engagements. It became harder to keep up with everything we had to do. It almost seemed I didn't have time to go to work.

I belonged to a men's prayer group. What an encouragement this was! There were so many women's Bible study groups operating in our area and Betty found them inspiring. But there was very little opportunity for men to learn from each other, study the Bible and pray together. As I met with these men each week, we discussed our feelings and attitudes, our joys and frustrations. We were open and honest with each other and came to trust one another.

Betty's vision had weighed on my mind for a long time. That uneasy feeling I always got when God was trying to tell me something, plagued me constantly. It was time to share the vision with a few of our Christian friends and have them pray with us about it. The whole idea of starting an organization for Christian counseling and encouragement seemed greater than I could tackle single-handedly. I needed to feel that other believers were convinced of its necessity too.

The men agreed to pray. Some were a bit skeptical at first. Others were very enthusiastic. Yet all promised to wholeheartedly seek God's opinion on the matter. We decided they should tell their wives too and as couples search to discover what God was saying.

One by one, their confirmation was expressed. These brothers and sisters in the Lord were certain that God wanted us to start an organization which would emphasize Bible-based counseling. They committed themselves to stand behind us in prayer and even gave some initial financial support.

We began making plans to set up the legal structure for such a ministry. I thought it would be a lot of red tape, but the

Lord led us to the right people at the right time. It was much simpler that I would have thought possible. We chose a board of directors to oversee the administration of the ministry—a group of men convinced of the importance of our task.

By this time, about a year and a half had passed since we had left our children in Brazil. We shared with them by letter what was happening, but we tried to be cautious about suggesting they return to help us. So when we received letters from Joann's family and then from John's that they were making plans to leave Brazil and return to the United States, we were a bit surprised. Actually we were not so very surprised because we knew nothing was too hard for our God! It would be another miracle to have the children near us again! How we praised God when Cleber and Joann and their girls, Sandy and Sylvia, and John and Sharon and their daughter Monica arrived home! We laughed and cried for joy!

Just a month or so after the children returned from South America, we received a phone call from our son Mervin, informing us that he and his wife Laurel were resigning from his position as youth pastor at a church in Ohio. They would be moving to Pennsylvania too.

God never does anything halfway! Had we tried to coerce our children into these moves, we know we never would have succeeded. Probably we would have ended up making everyone miserable. As it was, the Lord spoke to each one separately, convincing them that they were to leave their work and come to Pennsylvania to help us. We knew the vision had truly been from the Lord! We thanked Him for making it come to pass in His own time and way!

With the sudden arrival of three of our children and their families, we had to get busy. Legally, we were well on the way to establishing a nonprofit organization. But we had no idea where this ministry would be located. Betty had envisioned a place in the country and everyone seemed to agree this would be ideal for a counseling ministry. However, finding available land in Lancaster County was difficult and very expensive. We looked at a number of properties—camps, schools, farms— nothing seemed just right.

An acquaintance of ours drove past a property that caught his eye. He thought it looked like an ideal spot for the ministry in which he worked. It was not for sale, but he stopped anyway and began chatting with the owner.

"You wouldn't consider selling this place, would you?" he asked the owner rather doubtfully. He was not prepared for the reply.

"Well, now that you ask, I think I would consider selling. There's just my wife and me here now and it's kind of a headache looking after our apartment tenants sometimes. Yeah, I think I would sell it."

"Do you have any idea what price you'd ask?" our friend ventured, trying to hide his eagerness.

"Well, offhand it's hard to say. I'd have to think about it—but, well—maybe around $225,000.00.

Our friend made arrangements to return and look the place over carefully.

There was no doubt that the property was worth at least $225,000.00—probably much more! There was an elegant, historic sandstone house on the property, a gigantic sturdy barn and a rustic, six-unit apartment building, all nestled scenically on a wooded hillside. Altogether there were about thirty-two acres of land.

Our friend shared the discovery with us and invited us to join him when he returned to inspect the house and grounds more closely. We were excited, yet we had to stifle our eagerness, for we knew this other ministry would have first choice. Inwardly, we were hoping the Lord had finally brought us to the end of our search.

From the moment we began our tour of the Hopewell Forge property (as it is called locally), we felt a peace which we had not sensed anywhere else. There would be plenty of space for our counseling in the large house, and room to expand for marriage seminars and meetings in the bam. There would be living space for our children in three of the apartments, and the remaining three could be furnished and made available for individuals or families coming for more intense counseling. It seemed perfect!

We continued to pray. The Christian couples who had been praying with us all along, made it a prayer priority. Our family prayed.

The other organization decided against buying. Delighted, we began our own negotiations with the owner and inside of a month, people had donated the money needed for the down payment. When God wants something, the money will always be supplied. He owns it all anyway, doesn't He? He owns the cattle on a thousand hills! The Bible says, "The earth is the Lord's and everything in it, the world and all who live in it" (Ps. 24:1 NIV). We had never taken on such a financial responsibility in our lives, and yet we were not afraid, for it wasn't our problem—it was God's. We were certain He wanted this ministry started. It had been His idea from the beginning. So He would take care of it! Our job was simply to keep our ears wide open to hear His voice and carry out His instructions.

There was a lot of work to be done around the property. But people donated time, money, furniture, ideas and a lot of prayer! Two months after first hearing about the place, it was ready for occupancy!

So it was that in September of 1978, Abundant Living Ministries began! We settled into the new house and I quit my job at Farmers' Supply in Lancaster. Three of our married children moved into the apartment building shortly after. Unitedly, we set about the task of organizing a counseling ministry. All of us were resolved to prove that Christian families can live and work together, while growing closer to the Lord and to each other.

Gradually, each of us found the areas of ministry for which God had gifted us, and there was a smoothness in operating the organization which we would have never dreamed possible. Betty and I increased our load of counseling appointments and speaking engagements. Some weeks we counseled over thirty people and speaking engagements took us into more than a dozen states, plus Canada, Haiti, Scotland and, of course, Brazil.

Though the rest of the Charles family did not live at Abundant Living Ministries, they supported what we were doing 100 percent! Is it possible that the Lord put this all together? Sometimes we felt like we ought to pinch ourselves to see if it was really true or just a dream. The Bible says, "He is able to do exceeding abundantly above all we can ask or think, according to the power which worketh in us" (Eph. 3:20).

Through the power of His Holy Spirit working in our lives, God led us into a life of ministry we would have never dreamed possible!

Yet, when we saw the many people who came for help and left with the joy of Jesus and hope for the future, we knew it was not a dream, but reality.

Mary came on the verge of a nervous breakdown! She was raising three teenage sons alone. Her husband had divorced her and disappeared. She had not heard from him in over a year. Bitterly, she recounted all the wrongs her husband had committed. We listened patiently.

Then we told her kindly but firmly what we believed God wanted her to do. Even when the other person is 99 percent wrong, the offended party must assume personal responsibility for his (or her) reaction to that wrong. We asked Mary if there were areas of her own life, which she knew were not right. The Holy Spirit was faithful and He convicted her. She began crying, heartbroken.

It is so much easier for us to see mistakes in others. Mary could clearly see her husband's faults, but had been blind to her own. We pointed out from Scripture what a wife's responsibilities are—loving submission, honor, respect and obedience rendered to her husband—a gentle, winsome conduct, helpfulness and creativity. She lamented, "Oh Betty, I probably drove him out of our home by my selfishness and my nagging. Yes, I drove him right into the arms of that other woman."

We were glad to see her repentance—naming her sins. As Protestants we sometimes accuse Catholics of making too much ado about confessing sins, but we've gone to the other extreme and frequently take it too lightly. Often we hear, "If I did anything wrong, please forgive me." 1 John 1:9 says, "If we confess our sins He is faithful and just to forgive us our sins and to cleanse us from all unrighteousness." That means if we name our sins, He will forgive us.

As Mary confessed her sins, we knew the Lord forgave her and threw those sins into the bottom of the sea to remember them no more (Isa. 43:25).

Then Betty said, "Now let's pray and ask the Lord to send your husband home. We believe it's God's will for families to stay together!"

She looked amazed. "How do you know he's not dead? I haven't heard from him in over a year!"

Betty argued, "How do you know he is? Maybe he isn't!"

"But maybe he's married again!"

"Maybe he isn't!" Betty persisted.

Mary laughed and finally agreed to pray, asking the Lord to bring her husband back and to reunite their family.

"Now we need to exercise faith and act like we believe it." Betty advised. So Mary went home and told her sons about the counseling session. They got so excited they started to get the house ready for their dad. About a month later Mary returned.

"Betty, we're believing, but he didn't come back yet. What do we do now?"

"Just keep on believing! Don't give up!"

I heard a minister say he believes, when we get to heaven we will see how many answers to prayer were just around the corner, when we gave up. Before the dawn, it's always the darkest. Mary determined not to give up!

Just a few weeks later, there was a rap at our door. We looked up, startled, as a radiant couple entered our kitchen. It was Mary with her husband! He had come home, their pastor remarried them, and they were on their way home from their second honeymoon.

"I can't thank God enough that Mary found this place and got help!" her husband exclaimed. "She's a different person!"

"And what amazes me is how long he had put up with me the way I was," Mary admitted.

What a difference it made when she was willing to look at her own life and do something about it, instead of just blaming the other person.

These are the kind of people who get help!

Each week we have seen marriages like this one, reunited and families drawn closer together. Adults, teenagers and even children have found out that Jesus is a real Person! Christians have been encouraged to rekindle their first love for God, to get back into studying the Bible and applying God's principles in their lives! The results have been astounding!

There are always those who will refuse to relinquish control of their futures to God, stubbornly ignoring the fact that only He can make their future really happy and successful. We will continue to pray for these people. The hundreds of people who pray for Abundant Living Ministries and support it financially, encourage us to carry on. And as long as people are finding help, and as long as God says, "Stay here," we will keep on sharing what Jesus can do with those who come to us!

Jesus can do anything! When we look back over our lives, we only wish we could have found out how wonderful He is, sooner! Yet, although we regret those wasted early years, He made up for lost time once we surrendered to His leadership. The years which followed our receiving the baptism of the Holy Spirit have been just so jam-packed full of His love and His care and His awesomeness, that those bad years seem like a vaguely remote and unpleasant dream. The abundant life which Jesus gave us, has become our way of life. Miracles are our way of life—because they are Jesus' way of life and His Spirit lives in us!

How thankful we are for the practicality of God! He cares about the everyday routines, and it is the nitty-gritty, which He delights to penetrate and transform with His joy.

Jesus gained control of our lives in 1957 and He has never let us go! We have gone through times of little faith, questioning and unwillingness to trust Him. Yet in spite of us, He's kept on nudging, loving and working on us until we give in to His plan. And His plan has always proved to be best for us! We know His plan is best for every individual, every marriage and every family! That's what we want to share with everyone we meet, everyone who visits Abundant Living Ministries, and everyone who reads this book.

A man once remarked to me that he was so impressed by what I had done with my life. I was quick to clarify that comment.

"It's not me who has done anything," I declared emphatically. "It's the Lord who has done everything! "

He thought for a moment and then replied quietly, "Yes, that's true, but the Lord needed your cooperation!"

I can't help but think how wonderfully happy our lives can be when we just cooperate with God's plan—when we accept Jesus as our Savior, ask Him to fill us with His Spirit and then simply follow the guidelines He has outlined for us in the Bible! That's the kind of life we're striving to live each day through His power. It's a joyful and abundant life—filled with greater blessings that we ever imagined possible!

That's the abundant life He came to give to everyone who sincerely desires it! If He gave that kind of life to ordinary folks like us—He will do it for anyone!

One day, Jesus was walking along in a big crowd of people when He suddenly stopped and looked up at the branches of a nearby tree. There, perched precariously on one of the higher limbs, was a little man—someone who had wanted so badly to see Jesus, he had climbed that tree.

Jesus spoke kindly and tenderly. "Zacchaeus, come on down! I'm going to your house " (Luke 19:1-9).

We were just "little" people—ordinary folks, when Jesus came to our house! Things have never been the same!

It's our prayer that this same Jesus will go to your house too! When you want desperately to see Him, He will do that very thing!

EPILOGUE
The Lasting Legacy
John's Update

Many years have gone by since *Heaven on Earth Family Style* was first printed in 1980. There have been many great times and certainly some tough times, and through them all God has been so good! We have learned that the Lord isn't a security against the storms of life, but He is a perfect security in the storms! He hasn't promised us smooth sailing, but He has promised us a safe landing! We have seen time and time again that His Word is true and His principles are best for us!

Dad and Mom's ministry in Brazil left a lasting impact. The church they planted in the small town of Tabatinga is a thriving congregation today. Many of the people who came to the Lord on the coffee plantation moved north to the state of Rondonia because the government was offering very reasonable land to those who would cut down the jungle and begin farming. Today over 30 churches in that area trace their roots back to that coffee farm, where Norman and Betty Charles introduced them to a joyful relationship with Jesus.

Let me update you about Abundant Living Ministries. The small family ministry grew to include several other counselors plus an office administrator and support staff. Hundreds have volunteered their time and talents to help with projects ranging from repairs, construction, and lawn care to envelope-stuffing and office help. Dad asked me to serve as administrative director which allowed him and Mom to remain focused on the direct ministry of counseling and teaching.

Our nation is only as strong as its families—and families can only be strong when living by Jesus' guidelines. Consequently, ALM aims at strengthening marriages and families, using a variety of avenues to pass on what Jesus taught.

We continue our original method of helping people through counseling. All sorts of problems walk through the doors: marital strife, parent-child conflicts, sexual problems, financial mismanagement. God has principles which apply to each situation and it is thrilling to see Him work in the lives of those who truly seek to obey Him. One husband who came for counseling wrote to us later with this report:

"I can't begin to tell you what your counseling has done for my wife and me! My wife asked for a trial separation because she wasn't sure she was committed to our marriage. We came for counseling and now that is all changed! My wife is committed to our marriage for the first time ever! I didn't write to you immediately because I wanted to see if this would last. And it has lasted! We find ourselves witnessing to others about the power of God and what He did for us. It is really exciting!"

The success of the counseling is not due to any sophisticated techniques. It's because we point people to an incredibly high-powered God! He doesn't give up on us and He doesn't want us to give up on each other, either! Many people need to know that someone cares about them and is cheering for them! Our counselors do that and the results have been positive! In fact, we offer classes teaching others how to provide this type of help to the individuals God brings across their paths. Every Christian can offer hope and encouragement to a friend in need!

Over the years ALM developed various seminars and classes to strengthen families. Majoring on Godly parenting and marriage improvement, thousands have attended these enjoyable and practical sessions. One couple wrote:

"We've been married over 20 years, but were never happy until attending your marriage seminar. Now we are actually enjoying each other!"

A wife wrote, "My husband and I are both Christians but we were two stubborn people who argued so much and wouldn't give in. That day at the seminar seemed to break down the resentment and bitterness we had held in our hearts all those years we were married. A new peace and love has come into our home. We've never been happier. Oh how I thank and praise God!"

We also continue to enjoy many opportunities to speak and teach in churches and organizations. Wherever we go we see people who are hurting, yet we know there is hope in any situation when God is put in His proper place—as Lord of all!

In November of 1993, Dad and Mom celebrated fifty years together. Their children, grandchildren and great-grand-children held a dinner in their honor. Little did any of us realize that this wonderful evening of celebration with about 200 of Dad and Mom's friends, would be their last public appearance together. The very next day, Dad received a shocking report from his doctor that he was in the last stage of acute leukemia and probably had only four to six weeks to live.

Dad and Mom cried together and Mom—she wanted to pray immediately, asking the Lord for healing! Dad told her, "I know the Lord can heal me. He's healed me many times before. Yes, we will pray and, if the Lord heals me, I will be grateful. But I sense that this is my time and the Lord is going to take me home! You know I've been so eager to go!"

Two years earlier, Dad had a glimpse of heaven when his heart stopped following a heart catheterization. He had seen the Lord about to open the door to heaven and had said, "Lord, I'm willing to go to be with You, or willing to stay if You have more work for me to do." At that instant the medical staff revived him and he concluded God wasn't quite done with him yet. After that tiny peek into eternity, Dad was never the same. He longed to go to heaven, saying there were no words to describe what he had seen. He used to say, "There's nothing in this world to compare with what the Lord has waiting for us! I can't wait to go!"

So Dad had no fear of death. The doctors told us that he would very likely suffer terribly in the last days. We, of course, prayed that he would be spared from that pain although Dad said, "If I do have to suffer, it will help me realize all that Jesus suffered for me!"

Dad lived five weeks and two days from when he was diagnosed. Those final weeks were a lesson in how to die, just as his life had been an example of how to live.

Upon receiving the diagnosis, he immediately wrote a list of everything he wanted to accomplish before his death.

He talked with all his children and grandchildren, encouraging them to continue walking with the Lord and to serve Him faithfully. And he spent hours listening to Christian music, often singing along and especially enjoyed the songs about heaven!

But many of the items on his to-do list were of a practical nature. He hired a carpenter to make needed repairs in their house. He asked me to install a 4x4 post in the lawn and mount a bird feeder so Mom could enjoy the birds. The basement remodeling project was kicked into high gear. An electrician rewired the receptacles at the kitchen counter so Mom would no longer trip the breaker by plugging in too many things at one time. Dad had the car title transferred to Mom's name, and completed legal matters that most people never think of before death. He wanted to make everything as easy for the family as possible.

Not that it was easy for any of us. Mom struggled after the diagnosis, imploring God to spare her husband's life. But God gave her the grace to pray as Jesus had in Gethsemane, "Not my will, but Yours be done!" When she told Dad that she had submitted his life and death to the Lord, he said, "Oh thank you Betty! That means so much to me!"

We had precious times as a family during those last weeks. We laughed and cried together. Once, after we had all been laughing over one of his jokes, Dad said, "If people looked in the window right now and saw us laughing like this when I've been told that I will die in a few days, they'd think we're crazy!" But in fact, those who witnessed his behavior were blessed! Many told us later that Dad's attitude had enabled them to be freed from their fear of death.

Dad passed away peacefully on January 12, 1994. He did not hemorrhage as the doctors had predicted and required hardly any pain medication. He had told us, "I have experienced life in its fullest. And now, whatever death is, I want to be alert and aware enough to experience it fully." I am confident that he fully enjoyed his entrance into heaven!

Before he died, Dad had encouraged Mom, "Betty, keep on helping people!" And then he added with that wonderful twinkle in his eye, "And take advice from your children!" I guess he knew that without him around, his wife might need some watching over!

And so, after Dad passed away in 1994, Mom continued counseling and helping people, just as Dad had urged her to do. She missed him so very much and sometimes shared tearfully how she would give anything to be able to talk with him again. Yet, on her darkest days, she practiced what she taught others to do. She would say, "Some people don't have a good partner at all. I was abundantly blessed with a great husband—for 50 years, and have so many wonderful memories. Someday (and I don't think it will be too long) I'll see Norm again! Thank You Jesus!"

Mom often talked about heaven. One of her pet peeves was the absence of teaching on heaven in many churches. As a child Mom had once heard her preacher state emphatically that, "heaven will be just like being in church—forever!" That didn't seem very appealing to Mom. She always wiggled uncomfortably on the hard wooden benches and grew restless during the long, boring sermons. To a mischievous and energetic little girl, eternal church sounded horrible!

As an adult she studied the Bible to see what God had told us about heaven. She became convinced that, contrary to what she had believed in her childhood, heaven would be anything but dull. She eagerly anticipated meeting the Lord face to face. She dreamed about the beauty that would transcend anything she had experienced here on earth, and she was certain she would recognize loved ones who had gone on ahead...especially Norm. She encouraged those dealing with terminal illness to pray and ask the Lord for healing, but also to talk freely about heaven. "After all, that is where we all want to be, isn't it?" she would ask.

In spite of her longing for heaven, she put all her energy into the continuing ministry of Abundant Living. Sharon and I lived next door and worked alongside her for almost 30 years and would have to say that with Mom around, there was never a dull moment!

It seemed that after Dad died, Mom had an increased gift for instructing and encouraging women. She spoke at many women's retreats and those who attended benefitted greatly by her teaching. She always kept the ladies laughing and wasn't afraid to laugh at herself.

On the way to one of her ladies' retreats, she realized she had forgotten to pack perfume in her suitcase. So she stopped at a Dollar Store, ran in and purchased a bottle of cologne. Never one to use things sparingly, she doused herself and proceeded to the retreat.

Arriving at the hotel just in time for the first session, she took a seat near the front of the auditorium. As she eavesdropped on the conversation going on right behind her, she realized the ladies were commenting to each other about the strong odor of "skunk" in the room. Mom began sniffing and realized that she also could smell a skunk. "How could a skunk get into this fine hotel?" she wondered. Moments later, to her horror, she realized that SHE was the skunk the ladies smelled!

When it came time for her to speak, she laughingly confessed to spreading the annoying scent with her cheap perfume! The audience laughed hysterically. Later that weekend a few of the ladies presented Mom with a gift: a stuffed skunk and a bottle of expensive brand-name perfume. Little did they know, Mom had recently tried that exact brand and scent of perfume and really liked it, but felt it was too expensive for her budget! And now she was blessed with the very fragrance she had desired!

In her talks Mom encouraged women to quit blaming their husbands for their problems, but to begin living lives of faith and thanksgiving. We knew of husbands who would urge their wives to attend Mom's meetings, because "my wife always comes home a sweeter person!"

Mom didn't shy away from sensitive issues either—like sex! She said that, contrary to what some may think, sex was not part of God's curse on mankind! It was created by God and therefore was very good. She encouraged couples to choose to be enthusiastic about the things of God and, "Sex," she insisted, "is one of God's things!" She would quip, "God told us that whatever we do, we should do heartily, as to the Lord… He did not say 'hardly at all!' " We in the family sometimes held our breath, wondering what she would say next. Men and women alike would be in stitches over her stories, but she always managed to convey a powerful message in the midst of the laughter.

Mom was an excellent counselor as well. She was a good listener, but she didn't just listen. She wasn't afraid to give strong Biblical advice, even when she knew it wouldn't be received well by the client. There are hundreds (probably thousands) of couples who would attribute much of their marital happiness to teaching they received from Betty Charles.

Mom used to quote Mark 10:29 "... no one who has left home or brothers or sisters or mother or father or children or fields for me and the gospel will fail to receive a hundred times as much in this present age (homes, brothers, sisters, mothers, children and fields – and with them, persecutions) and in the age to come, eternal life." She liked to remind people that trials were bound to come to any follower of Jesus. She would laughingly say, "You haven't had any problems yet? Don't worry. They will come!"

When problems seemed especially overwhelming, she would remind herself and others that, "just before the dawn, it's the darkest." And, "I believe when we get to heaven we'll be amazed at how many answers to prayer were right around the corner when we gave up!" Mom would never give up and she inspired faith in all who knew her.

Without a doubt, Sharon and I were influenced more by Dad and Mom than by any other individuals. Their example taught us to expect God to work supernaturally in our day-to-day routines.

At supper one evening, I told Sharon I had been noticing that the large Abundant Living sign by the highway was weathered and looking downright shabby. "We need a new sign, but the ministry doesn't have the funds right now to purchase one," I explained to her.

"How about we take a drive after supper, looking at signs? We can at least figure out the type of sign we want, when the Lord supplies the money," she suggested.

We drove all around that evening, looking at many styles of signs. The one that clearly caught our attention seemed just the right style for ALM's historic property. It was beautiful, with recessed lettering and gold-leaf paint. It was also obviously an expensive sign!

A few days after our scouting expedition, a businessman I had not heard from in several years phoned me. "John," he began, "my wife and I were driving past ALM last week and I commented to my wife, 'Honey, I believe those folks could use a new sign!' I get a lot of signs made for my business. You just go over to Eckert Signs in Ephrata and order a sign. I told them to expect you and asked them to send me the bill." I was thrilled with his offer but immediately recognized I would be hesitant to order the expensive sign we had admired on our drive. Imagine my further surprise when he continued, "John, you may order any style you want but I recently noticed a sign that I think would be the perfect fit for your place." You guessed it—he named the exact sign Sharon and I had selected!

One evening as I left the office and walked across the parking lot toward the house, I noticed that the white painted parking stripes had faded and were barely visible. I had been pleased with the low cost of the original striping job and further pleased that the white stripes had lasted so long. But I couldn't remember the name of the man or business who had done that job 10 years earlier. "I suppose I have an old invoice somewhere," I thought, "but it could take me hours of going through old records to find the information." I didn't relish the idea.

The very next morning, at about 8:00, my secretary buzzed me on the intercom, telling me a man had stopped by, asking to talk to me. As I entered the lobby to greet him, he extended his hand to shake mine. "Mr. Charles, you may not remember me but I did the striping on the parking lot some years back and was just thinking that you might be ready for fresh white lines, so I stopped in." Amazing! I call these events "God stories!"

One evening months later, we had a torrential rain storm. It sounded like a waterfall as the rainwater poured down the hillside, across the parking lot and began to flood the basement of the six-unit apartment building. I received a frantic call from one of the tenants informing me that their lower level was filling up with water. I rushed over and, along with several other neighbors, began wading through the water, carrying their belongings and furniture upstairs. By morning the water had subsided, leaving a muddy, absolutely horrible mess. Our son Tim took off work and together we were using shovels to scoop and scrape the muck from the floor.

Mid-morning we were called over to our kitchen for a breakfast sandwich. We discussed strategies, deciding the next step would be to use the garden hose inside the basement apartment. More water! My biggest concern was mold developing, knowing the water had been 18 inches deep in that dwelling area.

"What we really need," I commented, "is somebody like Andrew Bailey. He's done storm damage and restoration work and would know how to deal with the wet carpet and moisture in the walls." The problem, however, was that I had not seen Andrew in years. I knew he had moved but didn't know where. I did not have his phone number. And I did not know if he still had the storm damage/restoration business.

Within two minutes (no exaggeration!) of making that statement, the phone rang. It was our secretary, calling from the next-door office, telling me that there was a man in the office, asking to talk with me. "His name is Andrew," she stated.

"Andrew who?" I asked.

There was a brief pause while she asked the visitor for his last name. "Andrew Bailey," she replied.

"Before they call I will answer; while they are still speaking I will hear" (Isaiah 65:24). The verse rang in my mind, as I hurried out to greet Andrew. Turns out he had driven past the Abundant Living property that morning, a rare occurrence since his move. After driving past, he felt impressed that he should turn around, come back and ask me, "Is there anything I can do for you?" Can you believe it! Andrew was also blessed and encouraged to realize the he had heard God's instruction!

Sometimes a "God story" event is more than a blessing—it presents instruction or a special message! In March of 2010 I developed a serious internal infection, spending nine days in the hospital, then returning home to 30 days of self-administered IV antibiotic treatments, every eight hours around the clock. After a week at home, I reported to Sharon that it seemed the infection was gaining ground. I was feeling ill and, perhaps more significantly, quite discouraged. It just seemed as though God was not hearing our prayers.

The next morning I went downstairs to hook up for my 6:00 a.m. IV treatment. I was just organizing the tubes when I heard the sound of water running through a drain pipe—as when somebody on an upstairs floor flushes the toilet and you can hear the sound of the rushing water. But the sound didn't stop. "Hmm," I thought, "Sharon must be taking her shower but how have I never noticed how noisy it is downstairs when the shower is in use?" Just as I walked toward the location of the sound, Sharon called from upstairs, "John, what is that noise?"

I hustled to the basement and turned off the main water valve for the entire house. Back upstairs, I explained to Sharon that apparently a water pipe inside the wall had burst. Water was already covering the staircase landing and I figured there was plenty more inside the wall... somewhere. The wall, which extended from ground level the whole way up to the third floor, would need to be opened in search of the leak and then repaired. I went to my computer to search for a plumber who might help with the situation. I remember feeling quite dejected. With my chin in my hands, I pleaded, "Lord, I'm sure this is no big deal to You but I'm feeling overwhelmed with everything. And right now I don't have a clue who I can ask to come and fix this water line!"

I didn't have a clue who to call because Reynold (who was the ministry's standby plumber, electrician, carpenter... everything!) had informed me that he would be spending a month overseeing a disaster-relief project in another state and not returning for another week. Who could I call?

I finished my IV treatment, put the equipment away and headed upstairs. Looking through the kitchen-door window, I saw a service truck over at the far end of the ALM apartment building. It looked like Reynold's truck, but I knew he was away for yet another week! I asked Sharon to go check. Sure enough, it was Ren—he had returned a week early from his assignment and was working on a couple items on my normal to-do list.

Sharon asked him for help with the more-critical situation. I offered to turn the water valve ON, knowing he would hear the water and be better able to determine the location of the broken pipe. "Oh no," he instructed, "Let's not put any more water inside the wall." I was left wondering how in the world he's going to guess at where to break open the wall.

He tilted his head, analyzing, then scratching his head before taking out a tape measure. He took a measurement here and another there, then made a pencil-point mark on the wall. Using his utility knife, he cut a nine-inch square in the drywall, pushed aside the insulation and—the broken pipe was within an inch of being centered in the cutout!

I teared up as I said, "Ren, you have no idea what this means to me. Your steps were ordered by the Lord!"

Here's the message I received through this God story: "John, I have not answered your big prayer (which had to do with my health) the way you want. But I want to assure you that I love you and am watching over you. I have your back covered. Relax and trust me with both issues, big and small, health and water pipe." How comforting to know that HE has my back covered!

Coincidences? That's what some people would call these events. But there's been too many and way too often, in my life and the lives of my family, for me to accept that explanation. Jesus told his disciples, "If you, then, though you are evil, know how to give good gifts to your children, how much more will your Father in heaven give good gifts to those who ask him!" (Matthew 7:11). Sharon and I were discovering, as had my parents years earlier, the gracious kindness of our God.

I so enjoy telling these God stories. So, let me tell you a few more. These took place in Brazil, but after Dad and Mom's return to the USA. They astound me to this day.

Sharon and I were married a few years, living in Brazil, doing missionary work. Dad and Mom had returned to Pennsylvania about 10 years before.

They decided to travel to Brazil to visit us, as well as my sister Joann and her family. Upon arrival Mom presented me with a list of people she hoped they could visit. I scanned the list, recognizing that most still lived in the general area. Their visits would be easy to arrange. But there were two that wouldn't be easy—in fact one was probably impossible!

I learned the one family had moved several hours away. Directions to their location were sketchy but I told Dad that we could play detective along the way and perhaps be successful in finding them.

The second situation was the impossible one. I was told that Celestino and his family had moved to another state, leaving no forwarding address. Mom commented that surely we could drive to that state and look for them. This would be compared to a New Yorker wanting to drive to Ohio to look for somebody, with no address—and this was before internet, Facebook, or GPS! Dad and I both explained the impracticality of such an effort. Mom insisted. Dad rolled his eyes and then announced, "No, Betty, we can't do that."

Ever the optimist, Mom persisted, "Okay, but we can certainly pray, can't we?" Pray we did—"Lord, we would like to meet with Celestino and his wife but You would need to make it happen. Thank You, Lord!"

Now, going back to the first family—the directions I'd been given were very sketchy and by late afternoon we had left the main road and were driving on an isolated country lane, not certain that we were anywhere near our desired destination. We were now down to a cart path which took us through a section of woods, after which we bounced across a crude cattle guard, finding ourselves in a pasture surrounded by a barbed-wire fence. In the distance I saw a person standing by the fence. "Good! We can ask if he has ever heard of this family." Sliding open the window of the VW van, I greeted a teenage boy and began to ask if he knew of this family we were hunting. I was interrupted mid-sentence as the young man exclaimed, "I know who you are—You're Pastor Norman!"

I was caught off-guard, shocked, but then responded, "Actually, I'm not Pastor Norman. Pastor Norman is my dad, and he's seated here behind me."

"Yes, I know!" the teenager continued exuberantly. "God spoke to me in a dream last night and told me that Pastor Norman and Dona (Mrs.) Betty would be visiting today and that I should stand by the fence in the afternoon, to open the gate for them!"

Praise God! Ten years out of the country and absolutely no communication of any kind (other than the dream) had taken place with this family!

Now, that second "impossible" visit—Later that week Dad and Mom needed to travel to Curitiba, the capital city of the state where Sharon and I lived. They needed to settle some legal issues regarding their adopted daughters. Since they weren't very familiar with that city or the bus system, I offered to make the seven-hour overnight bus trip with them.

Around 3 a.m. our bus broke down. The driver coasted to a stop along the edge of the road. Since we were headed to the state capital, the road was a decent two-lane asphalt with significant bus traffic. Within a few minutes, another bus from the same company came along. Seeing us broken-down by the side of the road, the second driver pulled over to see if he could be of any help. Momentarily the cabin lights came on and the second driver addressed us passengers.

"I am also going to Curitiba," he stated. "My bus is full. Every seat is taken. However, if any of you don't mind standing in the aisle of my bus, you can come with me."

It seemed like a no-brainer. "Come on," I urged Dad and Mom. "It's only a few hours of standing and at least we'll arrive in Curitiba as planned." We were the first to board the rescue bus.

The driver had not turned on the interior lights in his bus so the three of us carefully groped our way down the aisle. All the other passengers from our broken-down bus followed our lead, resulting in us being pushed down the aisle, to the very rear of the bus.

The driver put the bus into gear and started off with an abrupt jerk. Mom lost her balance and fell with an ungraceful plop into the lap of a dozing passenger—a man! Totally embarrassed, she began apologizing profusely—"Desculpe. Por favor me perdoa!" ("I'm so sorry. Please forgive me!"). Her American-accented voice cut through the blackness. As she struggled to get back on her feet, the startled victim spoke out of the darkness, "Dona Betty… is that you? Dona Betty? It's me—Celestino!"

That's right! Mom had fallen right into the lap of the friend we had prayed she could meet. As it turned out, Celestino and his wife had, in fact, moved to another state but his wife was battling cancer and they had decided to travel to the large state capital to consult with a specialist. Celestino and his wife squeezed together, making room for Mom to sit with them. For the next several hours we were all able to chat and even pray together! Even as I write this I get chills, remembering that amazing night.

Okay—just one more God story. Dad had passed away. Sharon and I and Mom were continuing with the work of ALM. However, the country and people of Brazil always remained dear to our hearts. I led numerous short-term missions trips there and we often entertained Brazilian guests in our home.

Mom was in her 80's and, although in good health, we knew that international trips could soon become difficult for her. Offering to accompany her, I suggested that perhaps she ought to consider one more trip to Brazil while she was still feeling strong and fit. I further suggested that perhaps she would like to invite my sister Janete (the older of Dad and Mom's two adopted Brazilian daughters) to go along. Janete was delighted, especially since she had not been back to Brazil since her arrival in the U.S. at age 10.

As we planned for the trip, Sharon said to me one evening, "Wouldn't it be wonderful for Janete to be able to make contact with her biological sister?" I agreed and immediately called Janete, asking if she had any idea where her sister was living. Janete said she had not heard from her sister in over fifteen years. In fact, the last letter she had tried to send to her sister had been returned, marked "No such address."

"Do you still have that letter?" I asked.

"Actually, I think I did hang onto it," Janete replied. She called me later, giving me the last known address for her sister. Today we would try doing a search with the computer but such tools were not yet available.

Not wanting Janete to be disappointed, I didn't even tell her what I was trying to plan, but Sharon and I started praying that God would make a way for the sisters to be reunited.

I remembered one of my Brazilian friends, Pastor Périkles, telling me about a buddy of his who lived in Cascavel (the city of the sister's last-known address). I wrote to Périkles asking if perhaps his friend would be willing to do a little detective work. I provided the name of Janete's sister along with the last known address.

Weeks rolled by with no response and we concluded our efforts had dead-ended. Returning from church the Sunday before our scheduled trip, Sharon and I entered the house to hear our phone ringing. It was my Brazilian friend Périkles. "I have some good news for you!"

He reported that his friend went to the area of town where he thought that street was located. It was a poverty area and there were no named street signs so he thought he would start by simply knocking on some doors and asking if anybody remembered this person from years before. He greeted the first man who came walking down the street. Showing him a paper with the name of Janete's sister, he asked if the gentleman, by any chance, knew of her.

The man was startled when he looked at the paper. "Do I know her?" he replied. "She's my wife!" With some special arranging, we were able to speak by phone and make plans for the sister and her husband to both travel by bus, meeting us in São Paulo the next week.

What a sweet reunion! Both sisters had given up hope of ever seeing each other again. They cried and hugged and then cried and hugged some more! And I—I just had to shake my head again at God's kindness!

Do all our prayers get answered so dramatically? Of course not. There are things that we have prayed for, for years, which have not been answered in the way we asked. But that will not keep us from asking. We have a heavenly Father who loves His children. We will be bold enough to ask, but trust His wisdom enough to leave the answer up to Him.

That trip to Brazil, with Mom and my sister Janete, was wonderful. Back home, Mom kept busy with her counseling and speaking. Her prayer was that she could remain busy and active in ministry for the Lord right up to the end of her life. "Retirement" was a distasteful word to her. She had no intention of slowing down.

In January of 2007 Mom was asked to speak to a gathering of Christian counselors from the greater Lancaster County area. Although this event was hosted by ALM five times each year, it was the first time that Mom had been invited to address the group. She was asked to speak on the topic, "Keeping Christian Counseling Christian."

In her typical bubbly and hard-hitting way, she challenged the professional and lay counselors to expect God to work in the lives of hurting clients. She urged them to utilize God's Word and the power of the Holy Spirit to deal with people's problems. She pleaded with them to invite Jesus into their consultation rooms.

As she closed her talk that day, she said, "When Norm and I began counseling over thirty years ago, we were pioneers of sorts. There simply weren't many others providing the kind of service we offered. Now there are many… such as you, who are here today. I believe the Lord wants me to pray for each of you, asking the Lord to continue, through you, the important work of Christian counseling."

As the counselors filed past her, she prayed a special prayer of blessing for each one.

Sharon and I were standing toward the rear of the room, figuring that we would let the others go for prayer. After all, Mom could pray for us any day, so we didn't need to use up the group's time by also getting in the prayer line. But, as Mom finished praying for the last person in line, she asked, "Where are John and Sharon?" She proceeded to pray for God's blessing and anointing on us and our ministry. It was as though she were passing the baton to us and the others in the room. Little did we know just how significant that morning would prove to be.

A couple of weeks later, we were into the month of February—the time of year when ALM hosted a series of Sweetheart Banquets for married couples. With over two hundred people attending each evening, the dinners were wonderful opportunities to make new friends while providing special evenings of delicious food, lots of laughter, and a helpful challenge for husbands and wives.

Mom loved participating at these events and the audience loved her talks even more! When she arrived for our staff pre-dinner prayer, she seemed to almost glow.

A lady came up to the head table and told Mom how God had used her and Dad to improve their marriage. Mom teared up as she responded, "This means so much to me—to know that the Lord has used us to help others!"

When it came time for Mom to speak, I helped her up the couple of steps to the stage. She seemed a little shaky. And as she shared she seemed a little breathless at times. I doubt that people in the audience noticed it, but those of us who knew her well, noticed that she seemed tired.

Her talk was amazing! She had folks laughing at her jokes and, as she had done before the meal, she teared up a couple of times when saying again how blessed she felt, knowing that she and Dad had helped and encouraged marriages and families throughout her lifetime. She stressed the importance of being thankful—thankful for our spouse and for our family. She talked about faith—believing that God is working even before we see it—and thanking Him for the answer even before it has arrived. She urged the listeners to not take each other for granted but to use the time God has given them to show love to each other. There was a passion and intensity in her words that was extraordinary!

At the close of the event, Mom stood at the exit doors, shaking hands with the guests, even autographing some of her books. After guests departed, one of our children would walk with her over to her apartment (right next door to the ministry building). However that night she slipped out unnoticed during the commotion of the clean-up crew beginning their work.

When Sharon and I looked for her, we concluded that she must have been extra tired and simply decided not to wait for an escort to walk her home. We continued working with the volunteers, readying the room for the church service the following day.

Typically the group of volunteers would troop over to our house following the clean-up for some popcorn and "unwind" time. But that particular night, every worker said they needed to get home and so only our son Joel and Sharon and I headed to the house around 10:30 p.m. It seemed strangely quiet.

About 11 p.m. the phone rang. It was Mom. She said she was having excruciating pain in her back and wondered if we had Tylenol in the house. Sharon offered to take it over immediately, but it was such a frigid evening, I said I would take it. "Why don't we both go?" Sharon suggested and we hurried from our house, across the parking lot, to the apartment building.

We walked in without knocking to find Mom on the sofa, writhing in pain. Something was seriously wrong! I went to the phone and called the ambulance while Sharon dropped to her knees by the sofa, holding Mom's hand and praying for her. Within minutes she lost consciousness.

The ambulance crew could barely get a pulse or blood pressure. We told them that Mom had been diagnosed a few years earlier with an abdominal aortic aneurysm. She had just had her semi-annual check for that, and it remained unchanged in size. The doctor had explained to Mom that the risk of corrective surgery was greater than the risk of it rupturing, so she opted to not have the surgery. Now, the paramedics suspected almost immediately that they were probably dealing with a ruptured "Triple A" as they called it.

Sharon rode with Mom in the ambulance while I followed in our car. By the time I arrived at the hospital, Mom had regained consciousness and was able to talk a bit. The surgeon confirmed what the paramedics had suspected. He said that Mom was part of a very small percentage of people who survive a ruptured abdominal aneurysm long enough to get to surgery. He explained that Mom's only chance for survival would be immediate surgery.

"I never wanted to have this surgery," Mom said to us, "but I can't live like this. I will sign the permission for surgery."

"This is a very serious, major operation, Mom," we cautioned. "There's a possibility you might not make it through the procedure. But you survived long enough to make it to the hospital so we're going to pray for God's protection for you."

"I know that I might not make it," she responded. "But I'm ready to go or stay. I love you both. Please tell the other children and all the grandchildren that I love them!"

Although there had been a flurry of activity since arriving at the ER, those last minutes before she was wheeled into surgery were quiet. We were alone together and there was such a sense of peace. None of us knew what the next hours would bring, but we knew Jesus was there and that was all that mattered.

Following surgery, Mom spent the next three weeks in Intensive Care. We marveled at how God had answered Mom's prayer to be active in service to Him right to the end and then He tacked on those extra three weeks as His gift to the family.

A family member was by her side around the clock. We experienced precious times of praying, singing hymns, holding her hand and caring for her needs. It was a privilege and honor for us to serve this great lady who had poured so much into our own lives. My brother Mervin had been scheduled to leave on an overseas trip when Mom took sick. He canceled the trip and, since he had already cleared his schedule for three weeks, he volunteered to take the early-morning "shifts" each day, so as to be the consistent family contact person when doctors made their rounds each day. What a tremendous help he provided—his service was another demonstration of God's amazing attention to even small details.

Twenty days after her radiant challenge to 200 guests, Mom's doctors explained that, barring supernatural intervention, Mom was in her last hours.

Sharon came to me. "John—your mother often told me that she thought it was wrong for loved ones of dying family members to shy away from talking about death. She thought it was appropriate to pray for healing, but also to discuss heaven. If this is Mom's time to go, I think we should now be talking and singing about heaven. We should release her to go to her heavenly home."

The eight of us, who were present at that time, gathered around her hospital bed. Mervin prayed, tenderly releasing her to Jesus. We told her we loved her and sang hymn after precious hymn as we watched a life lived greatly here on earth slip quietly into the presence of her Great Savior.

Well over another decade has passed. We miss Dad and Mom—although we could never wish them back. Picturing them laughing together, enjoying the splendors of heaven and talking with Jesus face-to-face can't help but make us smile.

Sharon and I continue the work of ALM along with a team of wise, Godly individuals that the Lord has brought alongside us.

Although the Lititz property was sold to another ministry in 2015, ALM continues its counseling, teaching, prenatal classes, and instruction to lay counselors. In fact, ALM simply rents (from the new property owners) the very same counseling rooms we've been using since the old bank barn was remodeled into the ministry building, in the early 80's. We remain "right at home!" God is so good!

As I wrote at the beginning of this chapter, the amazing evidences of God's miracle-working power keep happening. By far the best of them all is when lives are changed, broken marriages are mended, hurting individuals are healed, and relationships restored. All of this because God is still God! He still does the impossible—more than we can ask or even imagine! He is the same yesterday, today, and forever (Hebrews 13:8)!

Dad chose a good title for his story, "Heaven on Earth Family Style." He and Mom left a lasting legacy of faith for their family and also for many others! I've come to recognize that heaven is a lot closer than most of us think. Yes, it is the amazing place we look forward to, when we die. Dad and Mom are enjoying that place today.

But as they learned during their lifetime here on earth, and as Sharon and I continue to experience every day, when Jesus lives with us and in us, we get a little taste of heaven right here and now. And that's definitely the best way to live!

About
Abundant Living Ministries

Abundant Living Ministries is a nonprofit organization registered in the state of Pennsylvania. Although not directly associated with a local church or denomination, all its staff are committed Christians, active in their local churches. The services offered by ALM are Bible-based and Christ-honoring.

Supported by gifts from interested persons, ALM aims to inspire people to apply God's principles, thereby experiencing the abundant life He intends for all.

A free newsletter, which announces upcoming events and offers encouragement for Christian marriages and families, is available on the website or by contacting the office.

Requests for more information, scheduling of appointments, and/or invitations for John or Sharon to speak at your local church, can be made by writing or phoning:

Abundant Living Ministries
541 West 28th Division Highway
Lititz, PA 17543
(717) 626-9575

email: info@AbundantLivingMinistries.org
website: http://AbundantLivingMinistries.org

Meadow where Jane,
the cow, was healed.

Wedding Day
November 27, 1943

Norm's family: (l-r) Norm, Amos and Susie (Norm's parents),
Ruth, Shirley

Betty's family: (l-r) Pauline, Betty, Ruth, Nora (mother), Phares Jr,
Phares Sr (father), John, Edna

In the early days: (l-r) Mervin, Betty, Jim, Joann, John, Marvin, Norm

Those who came to know Christ were baptized in rivers.

*In Campinas, bread, still hot from the bakery, was
delivered daily with a smile.*

Boarding the ship for second term of missionary service

The church on Fazenda Peroba coffee farm was often filled to capacity.

Home visits provided wonderful opportunities to share the good news. of Jesus!

Janete and Ivete were wonderful additions to the family.

Son John and Sharon, provide leadership to Abundant Living Ministries.

Betty's family: (l-r seated) Marvin & Ginny, Betty, Sharon & John;
(l-r standing) Laurel & Mervin, Janete, Joann, Ivete, Jim & Charlotte

The historic Hopewell Forge Mansion (built in 1740) became a
wonderful home for Norman and Betty's counseling ministry.